MASTERING ACTIVE DIRECTORY

DIRECTORY SERVICES, SECURITY, AND INFRASTRUCTURE MANAGEMENT

VICTOR P HENDERSON | ISSO-TECH ENTERPRISES™
CERTIFIED ETHICAL HACKER C|EH

ISSO-TECH PRESS™

MASTERING ACTIVE DIRECTORY

DIRECTORY SERVICES, SECURITY, AND INFRASTRUCTURE MANAGEMENT

VICTOR P HENDERSON
CERTIFIED ETHICAL HACKER C|EH

ISSO-TECH ENTERPRISES™

@ISSO.TECH.ENTERPRISES

MASTERING ACTIVE DIRECTORY

Directory Services, Security, and Infrastructure Management

COPYRIGHT © 2024 BY VICTOR P HENDERSON
CERTIFIED ETHICAL HACKER C|EH

ISSO-TECH ENTERPRISES™

229.320.151.8

TABLE OF CONTENTS

MASTERING ACTIVE DIRECTORY 2
TABLE OF CONTENTS 5
DISCLAIMER 8
INTRODUCTION 12
EPIGRAPH 16
ACTIVE DIRECTORY 20
SPECIAL THANKS 34
DEDICATION 38
CHAPTER | 01 40
ACTIVE DIRECTORY 40
CHAPTER | 02 56
PLANNING AND DEPLOYMENT 56
CHAPTER 03 72
INSTALLATION AND CONFIGURATION 72
CHAPTER 04 82
MANAGEMENT 82
CHAPTER 05 96
ACTIVE DIRECTORY RESOURCES 96
CHAPTER 06 106
SECURITY TACTICS 106
CHAPTER 07 140
ADVANCED SERVICES 140
CHAPTER 08 158
DATA RECOVERY 158
CHAPTER 09 174
CLOUD SERVICES 174
CHAPTER 10 192
ACTIVE DIRECTORY BEST PRACTICES 192

CHAPTER 11   200
DIAGNOSTIC TECHNIQUES   200
CHAPTER 12   218
PERFORMANCE   218
CHAPTER 13   228
REPLICATION   228
CHAPTER 14   238
DNS IMPLEMENTATION   238
CHAPTER 15   248
GROUP POLICY   248
CHAPTER 16   258
AD DATABASE ADMINISTRATION   258
CHAPTER 17   274
WINDOWS SERVER   274
CHAPTER 18   282
SECURITY & AUDITING   282
CHAPTER 19   294
POWERSHELL TECHNIQUES   294
CHAPTER 20   312
THE BOOK OF KNOWLEDGE   312
CHAPTER 21   328
DIAGNOSTIC BEST PRACTICES   328
EPILOGUE   342
BIOGRAPHY   346
ABOUT THE PUBLISHER   350

ISSO-TECH

VICTOR P HENDERSON | ISSO-TECH ENTERPRISES™
CERTIFIED ETHICAL HACKER C|EH

ISSO-TECH PRESS™

VICTOR P HENDERSON | ISSO-TECH ENTERPRISES™
CERTIFIED ETHICAL HACKER C|EH

DISCLAIMER

The information presented in **Mastering Active Directory** is intended solely for educational and informational purposes. While every effort has been made to ensure that the content is accurate, comprehensive, and up-to-date, the author and publisher cannot guarantee that the techniques and strategies discussed in this book will work in every environment or situation. The material in this book is provided on an "as is" basis, without any warranties, either express or implied. The reader is responsible for determining the applicability of the information to their specific circumstances and for ensuring that it is used appropriately.

Given the complexity and variability of IT environments, the author and publisher strongly recommend that readers conduct thorough testing in a controlled setting before applying any procedures, configurations, or recommendations from this book to a live environment. The guidance provided in **Mastering Active Directory** is meant to serve as a general framework; however, individual results may vary based on factors such as network architecture, organizational policies, software versions, and user behavior.

The author and publisher expressly disclaim any liability for any direct, indirect, incidental, or consequential damages that may arise from the use or misuse of the information contained in this book. This includes, but is not limited to, data loss, security breaches, or operational disruptions. Readers are advised to consult with qualified professionals, including IT consultants, legal advisors,

@ISSO.TECH.ENTERPRISES

and cybersecurity experts, to obtain tailored advice and solutions that address the unique challenges of their specific environments.

Furthermore, this book is not intended to replace professional training, certification programs, or hands-on experience. While it serves as a valuable resource for gaining a deeper understanding of Active Directory, it should be used in conjunction with other learning tools and resources. The author encourages readers to continuously seek out additional knowledge and stay informed about the latest advancements in technology, security practices, and industry standards.

By using the information contained in **Mastering Active Directory**, you acknowledge that you have read, understood, and agreed to this disclaimer and that you accept full responsibility for any outcomes resulting from the application of the material provided.

By viewing, or reading, this body of work, you hereby consent to this disclaimer and agree to its terms entirely.

Warning: The unauthorized reproduction or distribution of this copyrighted work is illegal. Criminal copyright infringement, including infringement without monetary gain, is investigated by the FBI and is punishable by up to five years in prison and a fine of $250,000.

THIS PAE LEFT BLANK INTENTIONALLY!

ISSO-TECH

VICTOR P HENDERSON | ISSO-TECH ENTERPRISES™
CERTIFIED ETHICAL HACKER C|EH

ISSO-TECH PRESS™

INTRODUCTION

Welcome to **Mastering Active Directory**, a comprehensive and authoritative guide meticulously crafted to empower IT professionals in managing and securing Active Directory (AD) environments with confidence and precision. In the rapidly evolving landscape of enterprise IT, Active Directory stands as a fundamental pillar, ensuring seamless authentication, authorization, and identity management across diverse organizational networks. This book is designed to meet the needs of a broad spectrum of professionals, from seasoned system administrators and cybersecurity experts to those new to the field, providing a deep dive into the intricacies of Active Directory.

Active Directory is not merely a tool; it is the backbone of IT infrastructure in countless organizations around the world. Its ability to centralize and streamline user and resource management makes it indispensable for maintaining the security, efficiency, and compliance of enterprise systems. As organizations grow and technology advances, the role of Active Directory becomes increasingly critical, necessitating a thorough understanding of its capabilities and potential pitfalls.

Mastering Active Directory guides you through every aspect of this powerful technology, from the foundational concepts of installation and configuration to the advanced strategies required for optimizing performance and enhancing security. The book is structured to offer a balanced approach, combining theoretical knowledge with practical, real-world applications. You will find detailed explanations, step-by-step instructions, and hands-on exercises designed to solidify your understanding and enable you to implement best practices in your own environment.

Throughout this book, you will also encounter expert insights and tips that reflect the latest industry trends and developments. Whether you are tasked with deploying Active Directory in a new environment, managing an existing infrastructure, or securing your organization's IT assets against emerging threats, this book provides the tools and knowledge you need to succeed. By the end of your journey through **Mastering Active Directory**, you will be equipped with the expertise required to tackle the most challenging aspects of Active Directory management with confidence and ease.

INTRODUCTION

VICTOR P HENDERSON | ISSO-TECH ENTERPRISES™
CERTIFIED ETHICAL HACKER C|EH

ISSO-TECH PRESS™

ISSO-TECH

VICTOR P HENDERSON | ISSO-TECH ENTERPRISES™
CERTIFIED ETHICAL HACKER C|EH

ISSO-TECH PRESS™

EPIGRAPH

EPIGRAPH | VICTOR P HENDERSON
ISSO-TECH ENTERPRISES™

"In the vast landscape of technology, mastery lies not in knowing all the answers, but in understanding the questions. Active Directory is the gateway to secure, efficient, and scalable network management. Master it, and you hold the key to the future of IT infrastructure."

- VICTOR P. HENDERSON -
CERTIFIED ETHICAL HACKER C|EH

ISSO-TECH

VICTOR P HENDERSON | ISSO-TECH ENTERPRISES™
CERTIFIED ETHICAL HACKER C|EH

ISSO-TECH PRESS™

229.320.151.6

VICTOR P HENDERSON | ISSO-TECH ENTERPRISES™
CERTIFIED ETHICAL HACKER C|EH

ACTIVE DIRECTORY

@ISSO.TECH.ENTERPRISES

ACTIVE DIRECTORY | THE HISTORY
INCEPTION TO MODERN-DAY ESSENTIAL

Active Directory (AD) is a cornerstone of enterprise IT infrastructure, playing a critical role in authentication, authorization, and identity management across global organizations. Since its introduction by Microsoft, Active Directory has become indispensable for managing network resources in complex environments. But how did this powerful technology come into existence, and how has it evolved over the years? This article explores the history of Active Directory, tracing its development from its origins to its current status as a key component in modern IT environments.

The Origins: Early Windows Networking

Before the advent of Active Directory, Microsoft's approach to networking and directory services was relatively rudimentary. In the early 1990s, Windows NT 3.1 introduced the concept of domains, where a primary domain controller (PDC) managed user accounts and security information for a network. However, the system had significant limitations, including a lack of scalability and complexity in managing larger networks.

As organizations grew, the need for a more robust and scalable directory service became apparent. The existing systems, including Windows NT 3.5 and 4.0, relied on the Security Accounts Manager (SAM) database to store security information. Although SAM worked for smaller networks, it was not designed to handle the increasing complexity and size of enterprise environments.

The Birth of Active Directory: Windows 2000

The demand for a more sophisticated and scalable solution led Microsoft to develop Active Directory as part of its Windows 2000 Server operating system, released in February 2000. Active Directory was designed to address the limitations of earlier systems by providing a centralized and hierarchical framework for managing network resources, including users, computers, and services.

At its core, Active Directory introduced the concept of domains, trees, and forests, allowing for a logical and hierarchical organization of network resources. This design made it possible to manage large and complex networks more effectively. Additionally, Active Directory supported the Lightweight Directory Access Protocol (LDAP), making it compatible with other directory services and enabling more flexible integration with various systems.

Key Innovations and Features

Active Directory's introduction marked a significant shift in how IT administrators managed their networks. Some of the key innovations and features that set Active Directory apart included:

1. **Centralized Management:** Active Directory allowed for centralized control over network resources, making it easier to manage user accounts, security policies, and access controls across the entire organization.
2. **Scalability:** The hierarchical structure of domains, trees, and forests enabled organizations to scale their directory services to accommodate thousands of users and devices.
3. **Group Policies:** Active Directory introduced Group Policy Objects (GPOs), which provided administrators with the

ability to enforce security settings, software installations, and other configurations across multiple computers in the network.

4. **Replication and Fault Tolerance:** Active Directory's design included built-in replication between domain controllers, ensuring that data was consistently available and providing fault tolerance in case of hardware failures.

5. **Integration with DNS:** Active Directory was tightly integrated with the Domain Name System (DNS), allowing for efficient name resolution and resource location within the network.

Evolution and Enhancements: Windows Server 2003 and Beyond

Following its debut in Windows 2000 Server, Active Directory continued to evolve with each subsequent release of Windows Server. Windows Server 2003 introduced several enhancements, including the ability to rename domains, improved replication, and the introduction of the Read-Only Domain Controller (RODC), which enhanced security in branch offices.

In Windows Server 2008, Microsoft introduced Active Directory Domain Services (AD DS) as a distinct role, further refining the architecture and adding features such as fine-grained password policies and Active Directory Lightweight Directory Services (AD LDS), a standalone directory service.

The Modern Era: Cloud Integration and Hybrid Environments

As organizations increasingly adopted cloud computing, Microsoft responded by extending Active Directory into the cloud with the introduction of Azure Active Directory (Azure AD) in 2013. Azure AD brought the familiar capabilities of on-premises Active Directory to the cloud, enabling organizations to manage identities and access across both on-premises and cloud environments in a hybrid model.

Azure AD also introduced new features tailored to the cloud, such as single sign-on (SSO) for cloud-based applications, multi-factor authentication (MFA), and integration with Microsoft's cloud services, including Office 365 and Azure.

In recent years, Active Directory has continued to play a vital role in IT environments, with ongoing updates and enhancements aimed at improving security, scalability, and ease of management. The shift towards Zero Trust security models, where identity is a key pillar, has further solidified Active Directory's importance in modern cybersecurity strategies.

Conclusion

Active Directory has come a long way since its introduction in Windows 2000 Server, evolving into a critical component of enterprise IT infrastructure. Its ability to manage complex networks, enforce security policies, and integrate with cloud services has made it indispensable for organizations of all sizes.

@ISSO.TECH.ENTERPRISES

As technology continues to advance, Active Directory's role is likely to evolve further, adapting to new challenges and opportunities in the ever-changing landscape of IT. Whether on-premises, in the cloud, or in hybrid environments, Active Directory will remain a foundational element in managing and securing network resources for years to come.

ACTIVE DIRECTORY AUTHENTICATION PROTOCOLS

Overview of Authentication Protocols

Authentication protocols are critical to maintaining the security and integrity of networks, particularly within Active Directory (AD) environments. These protocols serve as the backbone of identity verification processes, ensuring that only authorized users can access sensitive resources. For small businesses and IT professionals, understanding these protocols is essential for establishing robust security measures that protect against unauthorized access and data breaches. This overview will delve into the key authentication protocols commonly employed within Active Directory, highlighting their roles, functionalities, and relevance to modern IT practices.

One of the most widely used authentication protocols in Active Directory is Kerberos. Developed by MIT, Kerberos is designed to provide strong authentication for client-server applications through a secret-key cryptography system. In an Active Directory environment, Kerberos facilitates secure communication and helps prevent eavesdropping and replay attacks. It operates on a ticket-based system, where users are granted tickets to access resources after successful authentication. For IT professionals and network engineers, mastering Kerberos is vital, as it underpins many security features in Windows environments and is crucial for implementing effective access control measures.
Another significant protocol is NTLM (NT LAN Manager), which, while largely deprecated in favor of Kerberos, is still present in many legacy systems. NTLM is a challenge-response authentication protocol used primarily when Kerberos cannot be

@ISSO.TECH.ENTERPRISES

employed, such as in older applications or systems not integrated with Active Directory. Understanding NTLM is essential for troubleshooting authentication issues, especially in environments undergoing migration or integration with cloud services like Azure AD. Despite its vulnerabilities, knowledge of NTLM can help IT professionals ensure smooth interoperability across diverse systems and platforms.

In addition to Kerberos and NTLM, the LDAP (Lightweight Directory Access Protocol) plays a crucial role in Active Directory environments. LDAP is utilized for querying and modifying directory services, allowing applications to authenticate users against Active Directory. It operates over TCP/IP and is integral for managing users, groups, and other directory objects. Familiarity with LDAP is essential for system engineers and network administrators seeking to implement efficient user management strategies and streamline authentication processes across various applications.

As small businesses increasingly adopt cloud technologies, understanding the integration of Active Directory with modern authentication protocols becomes imperative. Protocols such as OAuth and SAML (Security Assertion Markup Language) are gaining traction due to their ability to support single sign-on (SSO) and federated identity management. These protocols enable organizations to facilitate seamless access to applications hosted in the cloud, while still leveraging Active Directory for user authentication. For IT professionals, mastering these modern protocols alongside traditional methods ensures a comprehensive approach to security and user management, ultimately enhancing the efficiency and resilience of their IT infrastructure.

VICTOR P HENDERSON | ISSO-TECH ENTERPRISES™
CERTIFIED ETHICAL HACKER C|EH

ISSO-TECH PRESS™

229.320.151.8

Kerberos vs. NTLM: Key Differences
Kerberos vs. NTLM: Key Differences
When it comes to authentication protocols within Active Directory environments, Kerberos and NTLM stand out as the two primary mechanisms employed for securing user identities and access rights. Understanding the key differences between these two protocols is essential for IT professionals, network engineers, and system engineers working with Active Directory, particularly in small business settings where security and efficiency are paramount. This subchapter delves into the distinct characteristics of Kerberos and NTLM, highlighting their operational methodologies, security features, and appropriate use cases.

Kerberos, a network authentication protocol, operates on a ticket-based system that enhances security through mutual authentication. When a user logs into a network, Kerberos issues a Ticket Granting Ticket (TGT) after verifying the user's credentials. This TGT can then be used to request service tickets for accessing various network resources without needing to re-enter passwords, thus minimizing the risk of credential interception. In contrast, NTLM (NT LAN Manager) relies on a challenge-response mechanism where the client and server engage in a back-and-forth exchange of hashed passwords. This design, while simpler, exposes NTLM to several vulnerabilities, including susceptibility to replay attacks and brute force attempts.

Security is a critical differentiator between Kerberos and NTLM. Kerberos employs strong encryption standards, making it significantly more secure against eavesdropping and man-in-the-middle attacks. Each ticket in the Kerberos system is encrypted, and the protocol supports more robust mechanisms for verifying

@ISSO.TECH.ENTERPRISES

the identity of both clients and servers. NTLM, on the other hand, uses less secure hashing algorithms and does not support mutual authentication. This lack of mutual authentication can lead to scenarios where an attacker can impersonate a user or service, undermining the integrity of the network.

In terms of performance and scalability, Kerberos is generally considered superior to NTLM, particularly in larger environments. Its ability to issue tickets and manage authentication requests efficiently means it can handle a high volume of users and services without significant performance degradation. NTLM, while still functional for smaller networks or legacy systems, may face challenges as the number of authentication requests increases. For small businesses looking to streamline their Active Directory tasks, implementing Kerberos can lead to improved efficiency and a more manageable authentication process.

Ultimately, the choice between Kerberos and NTLM should be informed by the specific requirements of the organization. For modern Active Directory environments, especially those integrated with cloud services or requiring stringent security measures, Kerberos is the recommended protocol. However, NTLM may still be necessary for compatibility with older systems or applications that do not support Kerberos. Recognizing these differences and assessing the context in which each protocol operates will enable IT professionals to make informed decisions that enhance security and operational efficiency in their Active Directory management strategies.

Implementing Secure Authentication Practices
Implementing secure authentication practices within Active Directory (AD) is crucial for small businesses and IT professionals aiming to safeguard sensitive data and maintain user integrity. The authentication process is the first line of defense against unauthorized access, and as cyber threats become more sophisticated, so must our strategies for protecting access to critical systems. In this subchapter, we will explore best practices for implementing secure authentication mechanisms in Active Directory, focusing on methods that can be efficiently automated using PowerShell.

One of the foundational elements of secure authentication is the use of strong passwords. Small businesses often underestimate the significance of password complexity and length. Implementing Group Policy Objects (GPOs) to enforce password policies can significantly reduce the risk of unauthorized access. These policies can require users to create complex passwords that include a mix of uppercase and lowercase letters, numbers, and special characters, along with regular password expiration intervals. Automating the enforcement of these policies through PowerShell scripts not only ensures compliance but also reduces the administrative burden on IT professionals.

In addition to strong passwords, multi-factor authentication (MFA) is an essential practice for enhancing security. MFA requires users to provide two or more verification factors to gain access, making it considerably harder for attackers to breach accounts. Integrating MFA with Active Directory can be seamlessly managed with PowerShell, allowing administrators to automate the provisioning and configuration of MFA settings across the organization. This integration is particularly vital in cloud environments, where users may access AD resources from multiple locations and devices, thereby introducing additional vulnerabilities.

Regularly auditing authentication logs is another critical component of a secure authentication strategy. By monitoring login attempts and access patterns, organizations can identify suspicious activities and respond proactively to potential security incidents. PowerShell provides robust capabilities for automating the collection and analysis of these logs, enabling IT professionals to generate reports that inform their security posture. Implementing a routine audit process not only enhances security but also supports compliance with various regulatory requirements, ensuring that small businesses remain accountable for their data protection efforts.

Lastly, consider the impact of user training and awareness on authentication security. Technical solutions can only go so far if end-users are not well-informed about security practices. Training sessions should emphasize the importance of recognizing phishing attempts and understanding how to use secure authentication methods effectively. By coupling automated technical solutions with comprehensive user education, small businesses can create a culture of security that empowers all employees to take an active role in protecting sensitive information. As the landscape of cybersecurity continues to evolve, prioritizing secure authentication practices will be a crucial step towards safeguarding Active Directory environments.

ISSO-TECH

VICTOR P HENDERSON | ISSO-TECH ENTERPRISES™
CERTIFIED ETHICAL HACKER C|EH

ISSO-TECH PRESS™

229.320.151.8

SPECIAL THANKS

I would like to extend my deepest gratitude to the many individuals and organizations whose support, expertise, and encouragement have been instrumental in bringing this book to life.

To My Wife: Your unwavering belief in my abilities has been a source of constant motivation. Your love, patience, and understanding have been the foundation upon which all my successes are built.

To My Mentors and Colleagues: Your guidance, insights, and shared knowledge have been invaluable. I am deeply thankful for the opportunities to learn from your experiences, and I appreciate the collaborative spirit that has enriched this work.

To the IT Community: This book is a reflection of the collective wisdom and innovation that define our field. I am grateful to the many professionals, educators, and industry leaders whose contributions have shaped the landscape of Information Technology.

To the Readers and Aspiring Technologists: Your passion for learning and desire to push the boundaries of what is possible inspire me. It is my hope that this book serves as a valuable resource on your journey to mastering the complexities of technology.

To ISSO-TECH ENTERPRISES™ Team: Your dedication and hard work have been crucial in making this project a reality. Your commitment to excellence, creativity, and technical expertise has been a driving force behind the success of this endeavor.

To My Publishers and Editors at ISSO-TECH PRESS™: Thank you for your professionalism, attention to detail, and tireless efforts to ensure this book meets the highest standards. Your partnership has been a cornerstone of this journey.

To My Friends and Supporters: Your encouragement and belief in my vision have provided the fuel necessary to complete this project. I am forever grateful for your support and friendship.

Finally, to all those who have walked this path with me, both named and unnamed, your contributions have not gone unnoticed. This book is a testament to the power of collaboration, perseverance, and the shared pursuit of knowledge. Thank you.

THIS PAGE LEFT BLANK INTENTIONALLY!

ISSO-TECH

VICTOR P HENDERSON | ISSO-TECH ENTERPRISES™
CERTIFIED ETHICAL HACKER C|EH

ISSO-TECH PRESS™

DEDICATION

THIS BOOK IS DEDICATED IN THE LOVING MEMORY
OF MY MOTHER

ISSO-TECH

VICTOR P HENDERSON | ISSO-TECH ENTERPRISES™
CERTIFIED ETHICAL HACKER C|EH

ISSO-TECH PRESS™

229.320.151.8

CHAPTER | 01
ACTIVE DIRECTORY

CHAPTER O1 || ACTIVE DIRECTORY INTRODUCTION
ACTIVE DIRECTORY ARCHITECHTURE

Overview of Active Directory
Active Directory (AD) is a directory service developed by Microsoft for Windows domain networks. It is a centralized database that stores information about network resources such as computers, users, groups, printers, and more. Active Directory provides a way to organize and manage this information, making it easier for administrators to control access and enforce security policies across the network.

Key components of Active Directory include:
1. Domain: A domain is a logical grouping of network objects (computers, users, devices) that share a centralized database. Domains provide a way to organize and manage resources within a network.

2. **Domain Controller:** A domain controller (DC) is a server that manages security authentication requests within a domain. It is responsible for authenticating users, granting access to resources, and enforcing security policies.

3. **Organizational Units (OUs):** OUs are containers within a domain that allow administrators to organize and manage objects in a more granular way. OUs can have their own security policies and administrative rights.

4. **Group Policy:** Group Policy is a feature of Active Directory that allows administrators to enforce settings and restrictions across a

ISSO-TECH PRESS™

network. This can include security settings, desktop configurations, and more.

5. **Trust Relationships:** Trust relationships are established between domains to allow users in one domain to access resources in another. Trusts can be one-way or two-way, and they help facilitate collaboration and resource sharing between domains.

6. **LDAP:** Active Directory uses the Lightweight Directory Access Protocol (LDAP) to provide access to its database. LDAP is a standard protocol used for accessing and managing directory services.

Active Directory plays a crucial role in managing and securing Windows networks. It provides a centralized way to manage users, resources, and security policies, making it an essential tool for network administrators.

Evolution and history
Active Directory (AD) has evolved significantly since its inception, adapting to the changing needs of modern IT environments. Here is an overview of the evolution of Active Directory:

1. **Windows NT 3.1 Directory Service** - The first version of a directory service for Windows was introduced in Windows NT 3.1. It was a basic directory service with limited capabilities compared to later versions of Active Directory.

@ISSO.TECH.ENTERPRISES

2. **Windows NT 4.0 Domain Model** - With the release of Windows NT 4.0, Microsoft introduced the concept of domains and domain controllers. This model allowed for centralized user and resource management within a domain.

3. **Windows 2000 Active Directory** - Active Directory as we know it today was introduced with Windows 2000 Server. This version introduced a hierarchical directory structure, support for multiple domains, and improved scalability and security features.

4. Windows Server 2003 - Windows Server 2003 built upon the foundation of Active Directory in Windows 2000, adding features such as the ability to rename domains and domain controllers, as well as the introduction of the shadow copy feature for Active Directory.

5. **Windows Server 2008** - Windows Server 2008 introduced several enhancements to Active Directory, including the Read-Only Domain Controller (RODC) feature, which provides a more secure option for deploying domain controllers in remote locations.

6. **Windows Server 2012** - Windows Server 2012 further enhanced Active Directory with features such as the Active Directory Administrative Center, fine-grained password policies, and the ability to clone domain controllers.

7. **Windows Server 2016** - Windows Server 2016 continued to improve Active Directory, introducing features such as Privileged Access Management (PAM), which helps organizations manage and monitor access to privileged accounts.

8. Windows Server 2019 - Windows Server 2019 introduced additional security features for Active Directory, such as the ability to enable LDAPS (LDAP over SSL/TLS) by default and enhancements to the Active Directory Recycle Bin feature.

9. Windows Server 2022 - The latest version of Windows Server continues to improve Active Directory with features such as Active Directory Integrated DNS and enhancements to Active Directory Federation Services (AD FS) for better authentication and authorization capabilities.

Overall, the evolution of Active Directory has been marked by a focus on scalability, security, and ease of management, making it a powerful tool for managing and securing Windows-based networks.
- Core components and architecture

The core components and architecture of Microsoft Active Directory (AD) are essential for understanding how AD functions within a Windows network environment. Here is an overview of the core components and architecture:

1. **Domains:** A domain is a logical grouping of network objects (computers, users, devices) that share a centralized database, known as the directory database. Domains are used to manage and organize network resources and to enforce security policies.

2. **Domain Controllers:** Domain controllers (DCs) are servers that manage security authentication requests within a domain. They store a copy of the directory database and are responsible for authenticating users, granting access to resources, and enforcing security policies within the domain.

@ISSO.TECH.ENTERPRISES

3. **Active Directory Database:** The Active Directory database is a hierarchical database that stores information about network objects such as users, groups, computers, and printers. It uses the Extensible Storage Engine (ESE) as its underlying database engine.

4. **Organizational Units (OUs):** OUs are containers within a domain that allow administrators to organize and manage objects in a more granular way. OUs can have their own security policies and administrative rights, allowing for greater flexibility in managing network resources.

5. **Group Policy:** Group Policy is a feature of Active Directory that allows administrators to enforce settings and restrictions across a network. This can include security settings, desktop configurations, and more. Group Policy objects (GPOs) are linked to OUs and are applied to objects within those OUs.

6. **Trust Relationships:** Trust relationships are established between domains to allow users in one domain to access resources in another. Trusts can be one-way or two-way, and they help facilitate collaboration and resource sharing between domains.

7. **Schema:** The schema defines the structure and attributes of objects that can be stored in the Active Directory database. It determines what types of objects can be created and what properties those objects can have.

8. **Global Catalog:** The global catalog is a distributed data repository that contains a partial replica of all objects in the forest. It is used to facilitate searches for objects across multiple domains in a forest.

9. **Sites and Replication:** Sites are physical or logical groupings of network objects that are used to optimize replication traffic between domain controllers. Replication is the process of keeping the directory database synchronized between domain controllers.

10. **DNS Integration:** Active Directory relies heavily on DNS (Domain Name System) for name resolution. DNS is used to locate domain controllers, locate other network resources, and facilitate communication between clients and servers.

Overall, the core components and architecture of Active Directory are designed to provide a scalable, secure, and manageable directory service for Windows-based networks.

Understanding Active Directory Architecture

Understanding the architecture of Active Directory (AD) is crucial for IT professionals, network engineers, and system engineers in small businesses seeking to optimize their IT environments. Active Directory serves as a centralized directory service that facilitates resource management, user authentication, and security in a networked environment. By grasping its underlying architecture, professionals can better leverage AD's capabilities to enhance operational efficiency, bolster security protocols, and streamline automation tasks using PowerShell.

At its core, Active Directory is organized into a hierarchical structure comprising domains, trees, and forests. A domain is the fundamental unit within Active Directory, serving as a container for users, groups, and resources. Domains can be grouped into trees, which share a contiguous namespace, while multiple trees can be combined into a forest, representing the highest level of the AD hierarchy. This layered structure allows for efficient management of resources and simplifies the process of implementing policies across various domains, making it an ideal solution for small businesses with complex networking needs.

Understanding the role of domain controllers is essential in mastering Active Directory architecture. Domain controllers are servers that host the AD database and are responsible for authenticating users and enforcing security policies. They play a pivotal role in maintaining the integrity and availability of directory information. In addition, domain controllers can be configured in various ways, such as global catalog servers and read-only domain controllers, which can enhance the performance and security of the Active Directory environment.

Active Directory is also designed to support various protocols for authentication and communication, which is crucial in today's diverse IT landscape that includes on-premises, cloud, and hybrid environments. The Kerberos authentication protocol, for instance, is the default method used by Active Directory to ensure secure user authentication. Understanding these protocols is vital for IT professionals, especially when integrating Active Directory with Azure AD or managing group policies, as it allows for a seamless flow of information and improved security measures across platforms.

In conclusion, a solid comprehension of Active Directory architecture not only aids in troubleshooting issues and implementing migration strategies but also enhances overall security and compliance. For small businesses and IT professionals, mastering this architecture is an investment in the long-term efficiency and resilience of their IT infrastructure. As organizations increasingly rely on automation tools like PowerShell, understanding how Active Directory functions within this architectural framework will empower them to execute tasks more effectively and respond swiftly to emerging challenges in the realm of directory services.

Importance of Active Directory in IT Infrastructure

Active Directory (AD) serves as the backbone of IT infrastructure for organizations of all sizes, particularly for small businesses aiming to optimize their network management and security. It functions as a centralized directory service that enables IT professionals to manage users, computers, and resources effectively. By providing a structured framework for identity and access management, AD enhances operational efficiency and supports compliance with industry standards. This centralized approach not only streamlines administrative tasks but also fosters a robust security posture, essential for small businesses that may lack extensive IT resources.

The importance of Active Directory extends beyond basic user management; it plays a critical role in enforcing security policies through Group Policy Management. With AD, IT professionals can deploy security settings and software updates across the network consistently, reducing vulnerabilities and ensuring compliance with security best practices. This capability is particularly beneficial for small businesses that often face challenges in maintaining a secure environment. By leveraging Group Policy Objects (GPOs), organizations can automate the enforcement of security measures, thus minimizing the risk of human error and unauthorized access.

Moreover, integrating Active Directory with cloud environments, such as Azure AD, has become increasingly relevant as businesses migrate to cloud-based services. This integration allows for seamless single sign-on (SSO) capabilities and enhances user experience while maintaining stringent security measures. Small businesses can take advantage of this synergy to improve access controls and streamline the management of cloud-based applications. The ability to manage both on-premises and cloud resources through a unified identity platform not only simplifies operations but also prepares organizations for a more agile and scalable IT infrastructure.

Another significant aspect of Active Directory is its role in disaster recovery planning. For small businesses, the implications of data loss can be severe, making it essential to have a robust recovery strategy in place. Active Directory facilitates efficient recovery processes by allowing for the backup and restoration of user accounts, group memberships, and other critical directory data. Implementing a well-defined disaster recovery plan that incorporates AD ensures that businesses can quickly restore operations and maintain continuity in the event of an outage, thereby safeguarding their operational integrity.

Finally, the auditing and compliance features embedded within Active Directory provide valuable insights into user activity and system changes, which are crucial for maintaining security and regulatory compliance. IT professionals can utilize these features to track access logs, monitor changes to directory objects, and detect anomalies that may indicate security breaches. For small businesses operating in regulated industries, these capabilities are vital for meeting compliance requirements and demonstrating due diligence in safeguarding sensitive information. By harnessing the power of Active Directory, organizations can not only enhance their operational efficiency but also build a resilient and secure IT

@ISSO.TECH.ENTERPRISES

infrastructure capable of supporting their growth and evolving business needs.

Overview of PowerShell for Active Directory Automation

In the contemporary landscape of IT management, PowerShell has emerged as a vital tool for automating numerous tasks associated with Active Directory (AD). For small businesses and IT professionals, embracing PowerShell can significantly enhance operational efficiency and streamline workflows. This scripting language provides an extensive framework for managing AD objects, enabling users to execute complex tasks with simple commands. Understanding how to leverage PowerShell for Active Directory automation not only saves time but also minimizes the potential for human error, making it an essential skill for network and system engineers.

PowerShell's integration with Active Directory offers a rich set of cmdlets specifically designed to manage AD components such as users, groups, and organizational units. These cmdlets empower IT professionals to automate repetitive tasks, such as user provisioning and deprovisioning, password resets, and bulk modifications of user attributes. By automating these processes, small businesses can ensure that their directory services remain up-to-date and secure, ultimately supporting the organization's overall IT strategy. Moreover, this level of automation frees up valuable time for IT staff, allowing them to focus on more strategic initiatives rather than routine maintenance.

In addition to enhancing efficiency, PowerShell plays a crucial role in implementing Active Directory security best practices. By scripting security audits and compliance checks, IT professionals can proactively monitor the integrity of their AD environment. For

@ISSO.TECH.ENTERPRISES

instance, PowerShell can be used to identify dormant accounts, enforce password policies, and track changes to group memberships. These automated processes not only reduce the risk of security breaches but also ensure adherence to regulatory requirements, a critical aspect for businesses dealing with sensitive information.

The versatility of PowerShell extends to cloud environments as well, particularly in scenarios involving the integration of Active Directory with Azure AD. By utilizing PowerShell scripts, organizations can automate hybrid identity management tasks, such as synchronizing users and managing access controls across both on-premises and cloud-based resources. This capability is especially beneficial for small businesses transitioning to a cloud-first strategy, as it simplifies the management of user identities and enhances security posture in a multi-environment setup.

In summary, PowerShell serves as a powerful ally for IT professionals seeking to automate Active Directory tasks. Its capabilities not only streamline daily operations but also bolster security and compliance efforts. By mastering PowerShell, small businesses, network engineers, and system engineers can significantly enhance their Active Directory management strategies, leading to improved efficiency and a more secure IT infrastructure. As organizations continue to evolve, the importance of automating Active Directory tasks through PowerShell will only increase, making it an indispensable tool in the IT professional's toolkit.

ISSO-TECH

VICTOR P HENDERSON | ISSO-TECH ENTERPRISES™
CERTIFIED ETHICAL HACKER C|EH

ISSO-TECH PRESS™

CHAPTER | 02
PLANNING AND DEPLOYMENT

CHAPTER 2 | PLANNING AND DEPLOYMENT
MASTERING INFRASTRUCTURE CONFIGURATIONS

Designing an Active Directory infrastructure
Designing an Active Directory (AD) infrastructure requires careful planning to ensure it meets the organization's needs for scalability, security, and manageability. Here are the key steps and considerations for designing an AD infrastructure:

1. **Assessment and Requirements Gathering:**
- Assess the organization's current IT environment, including the number of users, computers, and other resources.
- Identify the business requirements for the AD infrastructure, such as authentication and authorization needs, group policy requirements, and data access requirements.

2. **Designing the AD Forest and Domain Structure:**
- Determine the number of forests and domains required based on the organization's administrative and security requirements.
- Plan the domain hierarchy, considering factors such as the number of users and resources, geographic locations, and administrative delegation requirements.

3. **Designing the OU Structure:**
- Create an OU structure that reflects the organization's administrative and business requirements.
- Consider factors such as delegation of administrative tasks, group policy application, and resource organization.

4. **Designing the DNS Infrastructure:**
- Plan the DNS namespace to align with the AD domain structure.

- Ensure that DNS is properly configured to support AD, including setting up DNS zones and records.

5. Designing the Site Topology:

- Define AD sites to optimize network traffic and replication between domain controllers.
- Consider factors such as network bandwidth, latency, and geographic locations when designing the site topology.

6. Designing the Global Catalog and Replication Strategy:

- Determine the placement of global catalog servers based on the organization's needs for authentication and resource location.
- Plan the replication topology to ensure efficient and reliable replication between domain controllers.

7. Designing Security and Group Policy:

- Develop a security strategy that includes authentication, authorization, and auditing requirements.
- Design group policies to enforce security settings, desktop configurations, and other requirements.

8. Planning for High Availability and Disaster Recovery:

- Implement redundancy for critical components such as domain controllers and DNS servers.
- Develop a disaster recovery plan that includes regular backups of AD data and procedures for restoring AD in case of failure.

9. Testing and Validation:

- Test the AD infrastructure design in a lab environment to ensure it meets the organization's requirements.
- Validate the design with key stakeholders to ensure it aligns with business needs.

10. Implementation and Deployment:
- Deploy the AD infrastructure according to the design plan.
- Monitor the deployment process to ensure that it is completed successfully.

By following these steps and considerations, organizations can design and implement an AD infrastructure that meets their needs for scalability, security, and manageability.

Domain controllers and global catalog servers
Domain controllers (DCs) and global catalog (GC) servers are critical components of an Active Directory (AD) infrastructure. Here's an overview of each:

1. Domain Controllers (DCs):
- DCs are servers that authenticate users, enforce security policies, and manage access to network resources within a domain.
- Each domain in an AD forest must have at least one DC, which contains a writable copy of the AD database for that domain.
- DCs maintain a replica of the AD database and use multi-master replication to keep the data synchronized with other DCs in the domain.
- DCs also provide services such as DNS, which is used by AD for name resolution.

2. Global Catalog (GC) Servers:
- GC servers are DCs that store a partial copy of all objects in the entire AD forest.
- The GC is used to facilitate searches for objects across multiple domains in a forest. Without the GC, each domain controller would

need to be queried individually for such searches, which could be inefficient.

- By having a partial copy of all objects, the GC can quickly respond to queries for objects in any domain within the forest.
- GC servers are particularly important for authentication and for locating resources in a multi-domain environment.

It's important to carefully plan the placement of DCs and GC servers in an AD infrastructure to ensure efficient authentication and resource location. Factors such as network topology, site connectivity, and user distribution should be considered when determining the number and placement of DCs and GC servers. Additionally, DCs and GC servers should be monitored and maintained regularly to ensure optimal performance and availability.

Site and replication planning
Site and replication planning is a crucial aspect of designing an Active Directory (AD) infrastructure, especially in distributed environments. Here's an overview of the key considerations and steps involved in site and replication planning:

1. Understanding AD Sites:
- An AD site represents a physical or logical grouping of one or more IP subnets that are connected by high-speed, reliable links.
- Sites are used to optimize AD replication and authentication traffic by defining boundaries for replication and client access.

2. Planning AD Sites:
- Identify physical locations of users, resources, and domain controllers (DCs) to determine the need for sites.

- Create sites based on geographic locations, network topology, and network bandwidth considerations.
- Define site boundaries to control replication traffic and client access.
- Assign subnets to sites to enable clients to locate the nearest DCs for authentication and service location.

3. Configuring Site Links:
- Site links are used to define the replication paths between sites.
- Create site links to connect sites that need to replicate with each other.
- Configure site link costs based on network bandwidth and latency to control replication traffic.

4. Configuring Replication Schedules:
- Configure replication schedules to control when replication occurs between DCs in different sites.
- Consider factors such as network bandwidth and latency, as well as the frequency of changes in the directory, when defining replication schedules.

5. Monitoring and Troubleshooting Replication:
- Monitor replication using tools such as Repadmin and Active Directory Replication Status Tool (ADREPLSTATUS).
- Troubleshoot replication issues using event logs, replication status tools, and performance monitoring tools.

6. Planning for Disaster Recovery:

- Implement backup and restore procedures for AD data to ensure quick recovery in case of data loss.
- Consider deploying additional DCs in different sites to provide redundancy and fault tolerance.

7. Review and Adjust:

- Regularly review and adjust your site and replication plan as the organization's needs and infrastructure evolve.
- Consider factors such as changes in network topology, addition of new sites or DCs, and changes in replication requirements.

By carefully planning and configuring AD sites and replication, organizations can ensure efficient replication, reduced network traffic, and improved user experience in their AD environment.

CORE COMPONENTS OF ACTIVE DIRECTORY

Active Directory (AD) stands as a cornerstone of identity and access management within many organizations, particularly for small businesses that rely on a streamlined IT infrastructure. At its core, Active Directory provides a centralized platform for managing users, devices, and resources. The primary components of AD include domains, trees, forests, organizational units (OUs), and objects. Each of these elements plays a critical role in ensuring that IT professionals can effectively manage user authentication and authorization, while also maintaining security and compliance within their networks.

Domains are the foundational blocks of Active Directory, serving as a logical grouping of network resources that share a common directory database. Each domain functions independently and can replicate its data to other domains within the same forest. This hierarchical structure allows IT professionals to design their networks according to their specific needs, whether that involves a single domain for a small business or multiple domains for larger organizations. Understanding the domain structure is essential for mastering Active Directory and implementing effective management strategies.

Trees and forests extend the capabilities of domains by allowing multiple domains to be grouped together. A tree consists of one or more domains that share a contiguous namespace, while a forest is a collection of one or more trees that may or may not share a namespace. This hierarchical design enables small businesses to scale their operations while maintaining a high level of organization and security. Additionally, the forest serves as a boundary for security and administration, making it an important consideration for IT professionals tasked with configuring and managing Active Directory.

Organizational Units (OUs) further enhance the organizational capabilities of Active Directory by allowing administrators to create subdivisions within a domain. OUs can be used to group users, groups, and computers based on various criteria such as department, location, or function. This flexibility not only aids in the delegation of administrative tasks but also facilitates the application of Group Policies. For IT professionals, mastering OUs is crucial for effective Active Directory management, as they provide a means to enforce security settings and streamline user management processes.

Lastly, objects represent the individual entities within Active Directory, including users, computers, groups, and printers. Each object has its own attributes, which can be manipulated through PowerShell to automate routine tasks and improve operational efficiency. By understanding the core components of Active Directory, IT professionals, network engineers, and system engineers can better manage their environments, implement security best practices, and prepare for future integration with cloud services like Azure AD. The knowledge of these foundational elements not only enhances troubleshooting capabilities but also lays the groundwork for successful Active Directory migration strategies and disaster recovery planning.

Active Directory Domain Services (AD DS)

Active Directory Domain Services (AD DS) is a critical component of Microsoft's Active Directory architecture, serving as the backbone for identity and access management in network environments. For small businesses and IT professionals alike, understanding AD DS is essential for effective management of user accounts, computers, and other resources within a domain. By leveraging AD DS, organizations can streamline administrative tasks, improve security protocols, and enhance compliance with industry standards. This subchapter will provide an overview of AD DS, its functionalities, and its significance in a modern business setting.

At its core, AD DS provides a directory service that stores information about members of the domain, including users, groups, and devices, and manages their interactions. The hierarchical structure of AD DS allows for efficient organization and retrieval of data, making it easier for IT professionals to implement policies and manage permissions across the network. With features like Group Policy Objects (GPOs), administrators can enforce security settings, deploy software, and configure user environments consistently throughout the organization. This capability is particularly valuable for small businesses looking to establish robust security frameworks without the need for extensive resources.

Security is a paramount concern in today's digital landscape, and AD DS offers a range of features designed to enhance the security posture of an organization. By implementing Active Directory security best practices, such as regular auditing, enforcing strong password policies, and utilizing multi-factor authentication, businesses can significantly reduce the risk of unauthorized access to sensitive information. Additionally, AD DS integrates seamlessly with various authentication protocols, ensuring that identity verification processes are both robust and user-friendly. This integration is crucial for small businesses that may not have dedicated security teams but still require effective protection against evolving threats.

With the increasing adoption of cloud environments, the integration of AD DS with solutions like Azure Active Directory (Azure AD) has become a vital consideration for businesses. This integration not only facilitates hybrid identities but also enables organizations to extend their on-premises Active Directory capabilities to the cloud. IT professionals must understand how to configure synchronization between AD DS and Azure AD, as well as how to manage identities across both platforms effectively. This knowledge is essential for maintaining operational efficiency and ensuring that users have seamless access to resources regardless of their location.

Finally, the importance of disaster recovery planning in Active Directory cannot be overstated. A comprehensive strategy for AD DS disaster recovery ensures that organizations can quickly restore services and maintain business continuity in the event of an outage or cyber incident. By leveraging PowerShell for automation, IT professionals can streamline backup processes, create recovery scripts, and conduct regular testing of their disaster recovery plans. This proactive approach not only minimizes downtime but also reinforces compliance with industry regulations, ensuring that small businesses can operate with confidence in their IT infrastructure.

VICTOR P HENDERSON | ISSO-TECH ENTERPRISES™
CERTIFIED ETHICAL HACKER C|EH

ISSO-TECH PRESS™

Managing Users, Groups, and Computers

In the realm of IT management, particularly within small businesses, effectively managing users, groups, and computers in Active Directory (AD) is crucial for maintaining a secure and efficient network environment. PowerShell provides a robust framework for automating these tasks, thus simplifying the complexities associated with user and group management. This chapter delves into practical strategies for leveraging PowerShell to streamline these processes, ensuring that IT professionals can optimize their operations and enhance productivity.

Managing users in Active Directory involves not only the creation and deletion of accounts but also the ongoing maintenance of user attributes and access rights. PowerShell offers cmdlets such as New-ADUser, Set-ADUser, and Remove-ADUser, which enable IT professionals to automate these tasks with ease. By implementing scripts that batch process user accounts, organizations can reduce the time spent on manual entry and minimize errors. Furthermore, automating user provisioning based on predefined policies can enhance security by ensuring consistent application of access controls tailored to specific roles within the organization.

Groups in Active Directory play a pivotal role in managing permissions and access to resources. By leveraging PowerShell, network engineers can automate the creation, modification, and deletion of groups, as well as manage group memberships effectively. The use of cmdlets like New-ADGroup and Add-ADGroupMember allows for streamlined group management, which is essential for maintaining security best practices. Establishing dynamic groups based on user attributes can further simplify management, ensuring that users are automatically assigned to the appropriate groups as their roles evolve within the organization.

Computer management within Active Directory is equally important, particularly in environments where a diverse array of devices is utilized. PowerShell facilitates the automation of tasks such as the addition of computers to the domain, configuring their settings, and managing their policies. Cmdlets like New-ADComputer and Set-ADComputer provide IT professionals with the tools necessary to maintain an organized and compliant computer inventory. This is especially relevant for organizations transitioning to cloud environments, where managing hybrid infrastructures can introduce additional complexities in device management.

Finally, integrating Active Directory with Azure AD presents unique challenges and opportunities for small businesses. PowerShell can ease the transition by automating synchronization tasks and ensuring compliance with organizational policies. By employing PowerShell scripts to audit and manage users, groups, and computers across both platforms, IT professionals can create a cohesive identity management strategy. The ability to seamlessly manage on-premises and cloud-based resources not only enhances operational efficiency but also strengthens security posture, ensuring that businesses can respond swiftly to evolving threats in a dynamic digital landscape.

ISSO-TECH

VICTOR P HENDERSON | ISSO-TECH ENTERPRISES™
CERTIFIED ETHICAL HACKER C|EH

ISSO-TECH PRESS™

229.320.151.8

CHAPTER 03
INSTALLATION AND CONFIGURATION

CHAPTER 3 | INSTALLATION AND CONFIGURATION
ACTIVE DIRECTORY BEST PRACTICES

Installing Active Directory Domain Services
To install Active Directory Domain Services (AD DS) on a Windows Server, follow these steps:

1. **Open Server Manager:**
- Launch Server Manager from the taskbar or by searching in the Start menu.

2. **Add Roles and Features:**
- Click on "Add roles and features" in the Server Manager dashboard.

3. **Before You Begin:**
- Review the information on the "Before you begin" page and click "Next."

4. **Installation Type:**
- Select "Role-based or feature-based installation" and click "Next."

5. Server Selection:
- Select the server where you want to install AD DS and click "Next."

6. **Server Roles:**
- Select "Active Directory Domain Services" from the list of roles.
- A dialog box will appear. Click "Add Features" and then click "Next."

ISSO-TECH PRESS™

7. Features:
- Review the features required for AD DS and click "Next."

8. AD DS:
- Read the information about AD DS and click "Next."

9. Confirmation:
- Review the installation selections and click "Install."

10. Installation Progress:
- Wait for the installation to complete. The server may need to restart.

11. Configuration:
- After the server restarts, log in and open "Server Manager" again.
- Click on the notification flag at the top-right corner and select "Promote this server to a domain controller."

12. Deployment Configuration:
- Choose the deployment operation (e.g., "Add a new forest" or "Add a domain controller to an existing domain").
- Enter the root domain name for the forest and click "Next."

13. Domain Controller Options:
- Select the domain and forest functional levels.
- Set the Directory Services Restore Mode (DSRM) password and click "Next."

14. DNS Options:
- Choose whether to install DNS if it's not already installed.
- Review the NetBIOS domain name and click "Next."

@ISSO.TECH.ENTERPRISES

15. Additional Options:

- Configure additional options such as the paths for database, log files, and SYSVOL.
- Review the summary and click "Next."

16. Prerequisites Check:

- The wizard will perform a prerequisites check. Resolve any issues if necessary.

17. Installation:

- Click "Install" to begin the installation process.

18. Completion:

- After the installation is complete, the server will restart.
Once the server has restarted, it will be configured as a domain controller with Active Directory Domain Services installed. You can manage AD DS using the Active Directory Users and Computers console and other AD management tools.
- Configuring domain controllers

After installing Active Directory Domain Services (AD DS) and promoting a server to a domain controller, you'll need to configure various settings to ensure your domain controller functions correctly. Here are some common configurations:

1. DNS Configuration:

- Ensure that the domain controller's DNS settings point to itself for primary DNS and to another DNS server (if available) for secondary DNS.
- Verify that the DNS server has the necessary DNS records for the AD domain, including the SRV records.

VICTOR P HENDERSON | ISSO-TECH ENTERPRISES™
CERTIFIED ETHICAL HACKER C|EH

ISSO-TECH PRESS™

2. Time Synchronization:

- Ensure that the domain controller is configured to synchronize its time with a reliable time source, such as an external NTP server.
- Verify that all domain-joined computers synchronize their time with the domain controller.

3. Network Settings:

- Verify that the domain controller has a static IP address.
- Ensure that the network settings (subnet mask, default gateway, etc.) are configured correctly.

4. Operations Master Roles:

- Transfer any operations master (FSMO) roles that were not automatically assigned during the promotion of the domain controller.
- You can use the Active Directory Users and Computers console or the command-line tools to transfer FSMO roles.

5. Active Directory Sites and Services:

- Configure Active Directory Sites and Services to reflect your network's physical topology.
- Create site links and ensure that replication is configured appropriately for your network.

6. Security Settings:

- Review and configure security settings, such as password policies, account lockout policies, and group policy settings.
- Ensure that security groups are appropriately configured and used to manage access to resources.

@ISSO.TECH.ENTERPRISES

7. Backup and Recovery:
- Configure and schedule regular backups of the Active Directory database, SYSVOL, and any other critical data.
- Test the backup and recovery procedures to ensure they work as expected.

8. Monitoring and Maintenance:
- Set up monitoring for the domain controller, including event log monitoring and performance monitoring.
- Regularly review and maintain the domain controller to ensure its health and performance.

9. Testing and Verification:
- Test the domain controller to ensure that it is functioning correctly.
- Verify that users can authenticate, access resources, and perform other necessary tasks.

By following these steps, you can configure your domain controllers to ensure they are secure, reliable, and efficient in managing your Active Directory domain.
- Managing Active Directory Administrative Center

The Active Directory Administrative Center (ADAC) is a management tool in Windows Server that provides a graphical interface for managing various aspects of Active Directory (AD). Here's a guide on how to manage AD using ADAC:

1. Open Active Directory Administrative Center:
- Launch Server Manager.
- Click on "Tools" in the top-right corner.

- Select "Active Directory Administrative Center" from the dropdown menu.

2. Navigate the Interface:
- The ADAC interface is divided into several sections, including a navigation pane on the left and a details pane on the right.
- Use the navigation pane to browse and select different AD objects, such as users, groups, computers, and organizational units (OUs).

3. View and Manage Objects:
- To view and manage objects, select the desired category (e.g., Users) in the navigation pane.
- The details pane will display a list of objects in that category.
- Right-click on an object to view or modify its properties.

4. Create New Objects:
- To create a new object, right-click on the container (e.g., Users) in the navigation pane and select "New" > "User" (or the desired object type).
- Follow the prompts to enter the required information for the new object.

5. Search for Objects:
- Use the search box at the top-right corner to search for specific objects in AD.
- Enter the search criteria (e.g., name, username) and press Enter to see the search results.

6. Perform Administrative Tasks:

- ADAC allows you to perform various administrative tasks, such as resetting passwords, moving objects between OUs, and enabling/disabling user accounts.
- Right-click on an object and select the desired task from the context menu.

7. Customize Views:

- You can customize the views in ADAC to display specific information or to organize objects differently.
- Click on the "View" menu to access options for customizing the display.

8. Review and Confirm Changes:

- Before making changes to AD objects, review the changes carefully to ensure they are correct.
- Confirm changes by clicking "OK" or "Apply."

9. Monitor and Manage Replication:

- ADAC allows you to monitor and manage AD replication.
- Navigate to "Active Directory Administrative Center" > "Sites" > "Inter-Site Transports" to view replication settings.

10. Exit Active Directory Administrative Center:

- To exit ADAC, simply close the window.
By using the Active Directory Administrative Center, you can efficiently manage various aspects of your Active Directory environment using a user-friendly graphical interface.

ISSO-TECH

VICTOR P HENDERSON | ISSO-TECH ENTERPRISES™
CERTIFIED ETHICAL HACKER C|EH

ISSO-TECH PRESS™

229.320.151.8

CHAPTER 04
MANAGEMENT

CHAPTER 4 | MANAGEMENT
USER AND GROUP MANAGEMENT

Creating and managing user accounts

Creating and managing user accounts in Active Directory (AD) is a common task for administrators. Here's a step-by-step guide on how to create and manage user accounts using the Active Directory Users and Computers (ADUC) console:

1. Open Active Directory Users and Computers:

- Launch Server Manager.
- Click on "Tools" in the top-right corner.
- Select "Active Directory Users and Computers" from the dropdown menu.

2. Navigate to the Users Container:

- In the ADUC console, expand the domain name in the navigation pane.
- Right-click on the "Users" container (or the desired Organizational Unit) where you want to create the user account.
- Select "New" > "User" from the context menu.

3. Enter User Details:

- In the New Object - User dialog box, enter the user's First name, Last name, User logon name, and other required information.
- Click "Next."

VICTOR P HENDERSON | ISSO-TECH ENTERPRISES™
CERTIFIED ETHICAL HACKER C|EH

ISSO-TECH PRESS™

4. Set User Password:

- Set a password for the user account.
- You can choose to let the user change the password at next logon and set password options such as password never expires or user cannot change password.
- Click "Next."

5. Review and Confirm:

- Review the user account details and click "Finish" to create the user account.

6. Manage User Account Properties:

- After creating the user account, you can manage its properties by right-clicking on the user account in the ADUC console and selecting "Properties."
- In the Properties dialog box, you can configure settings such as Account options, Profile, Organization, Telephones, etc.

7. Enable/Disable User Account:

- To enable or disable a user account, right-click on the user account in the ADUC console and select "Disable account" or "Enable account" from the context menu.

8. Reset User Password:

- To reset a user's password, right-click on the user account in the ADUC console and select "Reset password" from the context menu.
- Follow the prompts to set a new password for the user account.

9. Delete User Account:

- To delete a user account, right-click on the user account in the ADUC console and select "Delete" from the context menu.

@ISSO.TECH.ENTERPRISES

- Confirm the deletion when prompted.

10. Manage Group Memberships:
- To manage group memberships for a user account, right-click on the user account in the ADUC console and select "Properties."
- Go to the "Member Of" tab to view and manage the groups that the user is a member of.

By following these steps, you can create, manage, and configure user accounts in Active Directory using the ADUC console.
- Understanding group types and scopes

In Active Directory, groups are used to organize and manage users, computers, and other objects. Understanding the different types and scopes of groups is important for effectively managing permissions and access within your environment. Here's an overview of group types and scopes in Active Directory:

1. Group Types:
- Security Groups: Used to assign permissions to resources such as files, folders, and printers. Security groups can also be used as email distribution lists.
- Distribution Groups: Used only for email distribution and cannot be used to assign permissions to resources.

2. Group Scopes:
- Domain Local Groups: Used to assign permissions within a single domain. Domain local groups can contain user accounts, global groups, and other domain local groups from the same domain.
- Global Groups: Used to organize users who share similar roles or responsibilities. Global groups can contain user accounts from the

same domain and can be members of domain local groups or other global groups within the same domain.
- Universal Groups: Used to organize users and groups from multiple domains. Universal groups can contain user accounts, global groups, and other universal groups from any domain in the forest.

3. Best Practices:
- Use global groups to organize users who share similar roles or responsibilities within a single domain.
- Use domain local groups to assign permissions to resources within a single domain.
- Use universal groups to organize users and groups from multiple domains when you need to assign permissions or perform other tasks that span multiple domains.

4. Group Nesting:
- You can nest groups within other groups to simplify management and assign permissions more efficiently. For example, you can add a global group as a member of a domain local group to assign permissions to resources.

5. Group Membership Caching:
- Active Directory provides group membership caching, which allows member servers and workstations to cache group memberships for users. This can improve performance and reduce the load on domain controllers, especially in remote locations.
Understanding group types and scopes in Active Directory is essential for designing an effective permission structure and managing access to resources within your organization. By using the right types and scopes of groups, you can simplify administration

@ISSO.TECH.ENTERPRISES

and ensure that users have the appropriate level of access to resources.
- Implementing group policies

Implementing Group Policies (GPOs) in Active Directory allows you to centrally manage and configure settings for users and computers in your organization. Here's a step-by-step guide on how to implement Group Policies:

1. Open Group Policy Management Console (GPMC):
- On a Windows Server, open Server Manager.
- Click on "Tools" and select "Group Policy Management."

2. Create a new GPO:
- In the GPMC console, expand your domain.
- Right-click on the "Group Policy Objects" container and select "New."
- Enter a name for the new GPO and click "OK."

3. Link the GPO to an Organizational Unit (OU):
- Right-click on the OU to which you want to link the GPO.
- Select "Link an Existing GPO" and choose the GPO you created in step 2.

4. Edit the GPO:
- Right-click on the linked GPO and select "Edit" to open the Group Policy Management Editor.
- Navigate through the settings under "User Configuration" and "Computer Configuration" to configure the desired policies.
- Policies can be configured for various settings, including security settings, software installation, scripts, and more.

5. Configure Security Filtering (optional):

- By default, GPOs apply to all users and computers in the linked OU. You can use security filtering to apply a GPO to a specific group of users or computers.
- In the GPMC console, select the GPO, and in the "Scope" tab, click on "Add" under "Security Filtering" to specify the groups or users to which the GPO should apply.

6. Force Group Policy Update:

- To apply the GPO immediately to all users and computers in the linked OU, you can force a Group Policy update.
- On a client computer, open a command prompt and run the command: `gpupdate /force`.

7. Monitor and Troubleshoot:

- Use the Group Policy Results (GPResult) tool to check the applied GPOs on a specific computer or user.
- Use the Group Policy Modeling tool to simulate the application of GPOs to a specific user or computer.

8. Deploy Software using Group Policy (optional):

- You can use Group Policy to deploy software to users or computers in your organization.
- To do this, create a new software deployment package in the GPMC console and specify the software installation settings.

9. Review and Adjust:

- Regularly review your GPOs to ensure they meet the needs of your organization.
- Adjust GPO settings as necessary based on changes in your organization's requirements.

@ISSO.TECH.ENTERPRISES

By following these steps, you can effectively implement Group Policies in Active Directory to manage and configure settings for users and computers in your organization.

SMALL BUSINESS REAL WORLD SCENARIOS

NY Eclipse Marketing, Inc. is a fictitious company employing a total of 5,000 individuals across six distinct departments: IT, Marketing, Human Resources, Sales, Publishing, and Distribution.

Each department is led by a department head and is staffed with supervisors and hourly employees. Departments are equipped with their own resources, such as printers and scanners, while certain supervisory staff will have access to both shared and private resources.

The company also employs seasonal part-time and full-time workers and accommodates remote users located in various geographical regions.

Now that we have the completed scenario, let's setup the Active Directory Infrastructure…

Creating User Accounts

We'll first start by creating the user accounts for all the company employees.

Step 1 Open Microsoft Management Console (MMC):

From your management workstation, open a command prompt and type mmc, when the Microsoft Management Console opens, add the Active Directory Users and Computers snap-in to the mmc console.

Step 2 Connect to the Domain Controller:

Choose the Target Machine, this should be The Domain controller that you want to manager remotely from your Management Workstation. Click "**OK**".

Step 3 Create New User Accounts:

Select the "**Users**" container (Folder) and then right-click on the folder and choose **"New User"**. Complete all the required fields to add the first user; the users User name, Full Name, Description or Department Name.

Then, create a temporary password and select the "User must change password on next logon and click "Create" when done. Follow these steps to create user accounts for all users.

When you are done, click **"Close"**

NOTE: *For temporary or seasonal employees, you can select the "Expiration Date and Time" at the bottom of the user's properties.*

ISSO-TECH PRESS™

Creating Departmental User Groups

Step 1 Add a New Group:

Navigate and select the "**Groups**" container "Folder", right click and click on "**New Group**". Complete the required fields for the Group Name and Description.

Step 2 Add Users to the Group:

Click the "**Add**" button and add all required users for this group. Click "**Advanced**" and then click the "**Find Now**" button.

Select your users from the list, and click "**OK**" to add the users.

Step 3 Finalize the Group Creation:

Click "Create" and then "Close" once all users have been added. And you are done.

Creating Shared Resources

Step 1 Add the Shared Folder Snap-in:

Return to your MMC, click **file** "and select **Add Snap-in**". Add the "**Shared Folder snap-in**" to your mmc console. Choose your target machine and click "**Finish**" and then "**Ok**".

Step 2 Create and Configure Shares:

Select the "**Shares Container**" (Folder), right click and select "**New Share**". Follow the wizard to create all required shares and set permissions for each share by adding the "**Groups**" to the Shared Folder(s) Properties for each company department…

NOTE: For streamlined administration and enhanced security, it is advisable to add users to groups and then assign the groups to shared resources. This approach facilitates centralized management.

ISSO-TECH

VICTOR P HENDERSON | ISSO-TECH ENTERPRISES™
CERTIFIED ETHICAL HACKER C|EH

ISSO-TECH PRESS™

229.320.151.8

CHAPTER 05
ACTIVE DIRECTORY RESOURCES

CHAPTER 5 | ACTIVE DIRECTORY RESOURCES
MANAGING RESOURCES

File and folder permissions

File and folder permissions in Windows are managed using Access Control Lists (ACLs), which specify the users and groups that have permission to access the file or folder and the type of access they have. Here's how you can manage file and folder permissions:

1. Viewing Permissions:

- Right-click on the file or folder you want to view permissions for and select "Properties."
- In the Properties window, go to the "Security" tab to view the permissions.

2. Changing Permissions:

- To change permissions, click on the "Edit" button in the Properties window.
- Select the user or group for which you want to change permissions and click "Edit."
- In the Permissions dialog box, select the permissions you want to grant or deny and click "OK."

3. Types of Permissions:

- Full Control: Allows users to read, write, modify, and delete files and folders, as well as change permissions.
- Modify: Allows users to read, write, modify, and delete files and folders, but not change permissions.
- Read & Execute: Allows users to view and execute files and folders, but not modify or delete them.

- List Folder Contents: Allows users to view the contents of a folder but not access its files.
- Read: Allows users to view the contents of files and folders but not modify them.
- Write: Allows users to create new files and folders and modify existing ones, but not delete them.

4. Inheritance:
- By default, permissions applied to a parent folder are inherited by its subfolders and files.
- You can disable inheritance and specify custom permissions for a folder and its contents.

5. Effective Permissions:
- To determine the effective permissions for a user or group, right-click on the file or folder, select "Properties," and go to the "Security" tab.
- Click on "Advanced" and then on the "Effective Permissions" tab.
- Enter the name of the user or group and click "View" to see the effective permissions.

6. Taking Ownership:
- To take ownership of a file or folder, right-click on it, select "Properties," and go to the "Security" tab.
- Click on "Advanced" and then on the "Owner" tab.
- Click on "Edit" and then select the user or group you want to set as the owner.

7. Auditing:

- You can enable auditing to track when files and folders are accessed, modified, or deleted.
- Right-click on the file or folder, select "Properties," and go to the "Security" tab.
- Click on "Advanced" and then on the "Auditing" tab to configure auditing settings.

8. Group Policy:

- You can use Group Policy to centrally manage file and folder permissions for multiple computers in a domain.
By understanding and managing file and folder permissions, you can ensure that users have appropriate access to resources while maintaining security and privacy.
- Share permissions

Share permissions in Windows control access to shared folders over a network. They are separate from file and folder permissions, which control access locally on the computer where the files are stored. Here's how you can manage share permissions:

1. Viewing Share Permissions:

- Right-click on the shared folder and select "Properties."
- Go to the "Sharing" tab to view the share permissions.

2. Changing Share Permissions:

- Click on the "Advanced Sharing" button to open the "Advanced Sharing" dialog box.
- Check the box next to "Share this folder" to enable sharing.
- Click on the "Permissions" button to manage share permissions.

3. Types of Share Permissions:
- Read: Allows users to view files and subfolders within the shared folder.
- Change: Allows users to view and modify files and subfolders within the shared folder, but not to add or delete files.
- Full Control: Allows users to view, modify, add, and delete files and subfolders within the shared folder, as well as change permissions.

4. Combining Share and NTFS Permissions:
- When a shared folder is accessed over the network, the most restrictive permissions between share and NTFS permissions apply.
- For example, if a user has "Read" share permission but "Modify" NTFS permission, the user will have "Read" access.

5. Administrative Shares:
- Windows creates administrative shares (e.g., C$, D$) for each drive on a computer by default.
- These shares are only accessible to administrators by default, but you can modify their permissions if needed.

6. Access-Based Enumeration (ABE):
- ABE allows users to see only the files and folders to which they have access when browsing a shared folder.
- Enable ABE on the "Advanced Sharing" dialog box for the shared folder.

@ISSO.TECH.ENTERPRISES

7. Share Permissions vs. NTFS Permissions:

- Share permissions control access to shared folders over the network.
- NTFS permissions control access to files and folders on the local filesystem.
- It's important to configure both sets of permissions appropriately to ensure security and access control.

8. Effective Permissions:

- To determine a user's effective permissions on a shared folder, consider both the share permissions and the NTFS permissions.
By understanding and configuring share permissions, you can control access to shared folders over the network and ensure that users have the appropriate level of access to shared resources.
- Printer management

Printer management in Windows involves setting up, configuring, and managing printers and print queues. Here's a guide on how to manage printers in a Windows environment:

1. Add a Printer:

- Open "Control Panel" and navigate to "Devices and Printers."
- Click on "Add a printer" and follow the on-screen instructions to add a printer.

2. Manage Printers:

- To manage printers, right-click on a printer in "Devices and Printers" and select "Printer properties."
- Here, you can configure printer settings such as sharing, security, and advanced options.

3. Manage Print Queues:

- To manage print queues, open "Devices and Printers," right-click on a printer, and select "See what's printing."
- In the print queue window, you can view, pause, resume, or cancel print jobs.

4. Set Default Printer:

- To set a default printer, right-click on the desired printer in "Devices and Printers" and select "Set as default printer."

5. Printer Sharing:

- To share a printer, open "Printer properties," go to the "Sharing" tab, and check "Share this printer."
- Configure sharing settings and permissions as needed.

6. Printer Security:

- You can configure security settings for a printer to control who can print to it.
- In "Printer properties," go to the "Security" tab to manage permissions for users and groups.

7. Printer Preferences:

- Printer preferences allow you to configure default settings such as paper size, print quality, and color options.
- In "Printer properties," go to the "Advanced" tab and click on "Printing Defaults."

@ISSO.TECH.ENTERPRISES

8. Printer Drivers:
- Ensure that the correct printer drivers are installed on the computers that will be printing to the printer.
- You can download and install drivers from the printer manufacturer's website or use Windows Update to find drivers.

9. Printer Ports:
- Printer ports are virtual connections that enable communication between the computer and the printer.
- In "Printer properties," go to the "Ports" tab to view and manage printer ports.

10. Printer Deployment:
- Use Group Policy to deploy printers to users or computers in your organization.
- Create a Group Policy Object (GPO) and configure the "Deployed Printers" setting under "User Configuration" or "Computer Configuration."

By following these steps, you can effectively manage printers in a Windows environment, ensuring that users have access to the printers they need and that printing operations are efficient and secure.

ISSO-TECH

VICTOR P HENDERSON | ISSO-TECH ENTERPRISES™
CERTIFIED ETHICAL HACKER C|EH

ISSO-TECH PRESS™

229.320.151.8

CHAPTER 06
SECURITY TACTICS

CHAPTER 6: SECURITY AND AUDITING
SECURITY TACTICS

Implementing security best practices
Implementing security best practices is crucial to protect your organization's resources and data. Here are some key security best practices for Windows environments:

1. Keep Systems Updated:
- Regularly apply security patches and updates to operating systems, applications, and firmware to protect against vulnerabilities.

2. Use Strong Passwords:
- Enforce strong password policies, including complexity requirements and regular password changes.
- Consider implementing multi-factor authentication (MFA) for an added layer of security.

3. Implement Least Privilege:
- Use the principle of least privilege to grant users the minimum permissions necessary to perform their job functions.
- Regularly review and audit permissions to ensure they are appropriate.

4. Enable Auditing and Monitoring:
- Enable auditing of critical systems and resources to detect and respond to security incidents.
- Implement logging and monitoring tools to track and analyze system and network activity.

5. Secure Remote Access:
- Use VPNs and secure remote desktop solutions for remote access.
- Implement strong authentication methods and monitor remote access activities.

6. Encrypt Data:
- Encrypt sensitive data both in transit and at rest to protect it from unauthorized access.
- Use encryption protocols such as TLS for data in transit and BitLocker for data at rest.

7. Secure Configuration:
- Disable unnecessary services and protocols to reduce the attack surface.
- Configure firewalls, routers, and switches to restrict access to essential services and resources.

8. Regular Backups:
- Implement regular backup procedures to protect against data loss due to ransomware, hardware failure, or other disasters.
- Store backups in a secure location, separate from the production environment.

9. User Awareness Training:
- Educate users about security best practices, such as recognizing phishing attempts and reporting suspicious activities.
- Conduct regular security awareness training sessions.

@ISSO.TECH.ENTERPRISES

10. Incident Response Plan:
- Develop and implement an incident response plan to quickly detect, respond to, and recover from security incidents.
- Test the plan regularly to ensure its effectiveness.

11. Physical Security:
- Secure physical access to servers, networking equipment, and other critical infrastructure.
- Implement measures such as access controls, surveillance, and environmental controls.

By implementing these security best practices, you can strengthen the security posture of your Windows environment and better protect your organization's resources and data.

- Auditing Active Directory
Auditing Active Directory is essential for maintaining security, compliance, and overall system health. Here's how you can audit Active Directory:

1. Enable Auditing:
- In the Group Policy Management Console, navigate to "Computer Configuration" > "Policies" > "Windows Settings" > "Security Settings" > "Advanced Audit Policy Configuration" > "Audit Policies."
- Enable auditing for categories such as "Account Logon," "Account Management," "DS Access," "Logon/Logoff," and "Object Access" based on your requirements.

VICTOR P HENDERSON | ISSO-TECH ENTERPRISES™
CERTIFIED ETHICAL HACKER C|EH

ISSO-TECH PRESS™

2. Enable Auditing for Specific Objects:

- In Active Directory Users and Computers, right-click on the domain or specific OUs and select "Properties."
- Go to the "Security" tab, click on "Advanced," and then on the "Auditing" tab.
- Add the users or groups you want to audit and configure the desired audit settings (e.g., "Read" or "Write" access).

3. Enable Directory Service Changes Auditing:

- Open ADSI Edit and connect to the "Default naming context."
- Right-click on the domain partition and select "Properties."
- In the "Security" tab, click on "Advanced," then on the "Auditing" tab, and configure auditing for "Everyone" or specific groups.

4. Review Audit Logs:

- Use Event Viewer to review the Security event logs on domain controllers and other relevant servers.
- Look for events related to account changes, logon events, object access, and other audited activities.

5. Configure Auditing with PowerShell:

- Use PowerShell cmdlets such as `Set-AdObject` and `Get-AdObject` to configure auditing settings for specific Active Directory objects.

6. Monitor Changes with Third-Party Tools:

- Consider using third-party auditing tools that provide more advanced monitoring, alerting, and reporting capabilities for Active Directory auditing.

7. Regularly Review Audit Reports:

- Regularly review audit reports to identify and investigate suspicious or unauthorized activities.
- Use the data collected from auditing to improve security policies and practices.

8. Maintain Audit Logs:

- Ensure that audit logs are securely stored and protected from unauthorized access or tampering.
- Consider using a centralized logging solution for easier management and analysis of audit data.

By auditing Active Directory, you can improve security, ensure compliance with regulations, and maintain the integrity of your organization's directory services.
- Monitoring and troubleshooting

Monitoring and troubleshooting Active Directory is essential for maintaining its health, performance, and security. Here are some key steps for monitoring and troubleshooting Active Directory:

1. Monitor Event Logs:

- Regularly review the event logs on domain controllers for any critical or warning events related to Active Directory services, replication, and authentication.

2. Use Performance Monitor (Perfmon):

- Monitor key performance counters related to Active Directory, such as LDAP operations, replication latency, and database performance.
- Use Perfmon to identify performance bottlenecks and issues.

3. Monitor Replication:
- Use tools like Repadmin or Active Directory Replication Status Tool to monitor replication between domain controllers.
- Monitor replication status, replication errors, and replication latency.

4. Monitor Active Directory Sites and Services:
- Use Active Directory Sites and Services to monitor and manage site replication, including site links, connection objects, and replication schedules.

5. Monitor Active Directory Database:
- Monitor the size and health of the Active Directory database (NTDS.dit) using tools like Performance Monitor or third-party monitoring tools.
- Regularly check for database corruption and perform integrity checks if necessary.

6. Monitor Active Directory Backup and Restore:
- Ensure that Active Directory backups are performed regularly and that backup files are stored securely.
- Test the restore process periodically to ensure that backups are valid and can be restored successfully.

7. Monitor Active Directory Users and Computers:
- Regularly review user accounts and group memberships to ensure they are up-to-date and comply with security policies.
- Monitor user logon events and account lockouts for signs of suspicious activity.

8. Use Active Directory Administrative Center (ADAC):

- Use ADAC to view and manage Active Directory objects, including users, groups, computers, and organizational units.
- ADAC provides a graphical interface for performing administrative tasks in Active Directory.

9. Monitor Active Directory Federation Services (AD FS):

- If you are using AD FS for single sign-on (SSO), monitor its performance and health using the AD FS Management console.
- Monitor AD FS logs for authentication issues and errors.

10. Use PowerShell for Monitoring and Troubleshooting:

- Use PowerShell cmdlets to automate monitoring tasks and troubleshoot Active Directory issues.
- PowerShell provides powerful tools for querying Active Directory information and performing administrative tasks.

By regularly monitoring and troubleshooting Active Directory, you can ensure its reliability, performance, and security, and quickly address any issues that may arise.

ACTIVE DIRECTORY SECURITY BEST PRACTICE

Implementing Least Privilege Access

Implementing least privilege access is a foundational security principle that ensures users only have the permissions necessary to perform their job functions. For small businesses and IT professionals, this approach minimizes potential risk by limiting access rights and reducing the attack surface within an organization. In Active Directory (AD) environments, where user roles and permissions can become complex, it is critical to establish a robust framework for managing these privileges. By automating the application of least privilege access through PowerShell, organizations can enhance both security and operational efficiency.

The first step in implementing least privilege access is to conduct a thorough assessment of current user roles and permissions. This involves auditing existing accounts to identify privileges that exceed what is necessary for users to perform their tasks. PowerShell scripts can be utilized to streamline this process, allowing IT professionals to quickly gather data on user access levels across the organization. By identifying excessive permissions, businesses can begin to restructure their Active Directory to align with least privilege principles, ensuring that users only retain the access they absolutely need.

Once the audit is complete, the next phase involves creating or modifying role-based access control (RBAC) policies within Active Directory. This includes defining user roles and determining the appropriate level of access for each role based on job requirements. By leveraging PowerShell, administrators can automate the assignment and modification of permissions, which significantly reduces the risk of human error and ensures consistent application of security policies. Additionally, integrating RBAC with group policies allows for more granular control over user permissions, making it easier to enforce least privilege access across the organization.

Regular monitoring and reviewing of user permissions is essential to maintain the integrity of least privilege access. Active Directory environments are dynamic; users may change roles or leave the organization, which can lead to outdated permissions. Implementing automated scripts that periodically review and report on user access levels can help ensure compliance with least privilege principles. This proactive approach not only aids in identifying potential security vulnerabilities but also supports compliance with industry standards and regulations.

Finally, providing training and awareness for employees about the importance of least privilege access is crucial. Educating staff on security best practices helps foster a culture of security within the organization. Additionally, creating a feedback loop where employees can report unusual access requirements or issues can further enhance security measures. By combining PowerShell automation, regular audits, and employee education, small businesses can effectively implement least privilege access, thereby strengthening their Active Directory security posture and mitigating risks associated with unauthorized access.

Securing Active Directory: Policies and Procedures

Securing Active Directory (AD) is paramount for small businesses and IT professionals, as it serves as the backbone of network security in many organizations. Active Directory not only manages user identities and access to resources but also plays a critical role in enforcing security policies. Developing a comprehensive set of policies and procedures tailored to the specific needs of a business can significantly enhance the security posture of AD environments. This subchapter explores best practices for securing Active Directory, focusing on policies and procedures that are essential for mitigating risks and ensuring robust protection against potential threats.

A foundational element in securing Active Directory is the implementation of strong password policies. Organizations should enforce complex password requirements and regular password changes to reduce vulnerability to unauthorized access. Additionally, employing account lockout policies can deter brute-force attacks by temporarily locking accounts after a specified number of failed login attempts. These policies can be easily managed through Group Policy Objects (GPOs), allowing IT professionals to enforce security measures consistently across the network. Regular audits of password compliance can further enhance security by identifying non-compliance and reinforcing adherence to established standards.

In addition to password policies, organizations must implement proper user account management procedures. This includes establishing a clear process for onboarding and offboarding

@ISSO.TECH.ENTERPRISES

employees to ensure that access rights are granted and revoked appropriately. Role-based access control (RBAC) is an effective strategy for managing permissions based on job functions, allowing businesses to minimize excessive privileges. Regular reviews of user accounts and permissions are essential to detect and remediate any discrepancies, such as orphaned accounts or excessive rights that may pose security risks. By maintaining strict control over user access, organizations can significantly reduce the attack surface within their Active Directory environment.

Incident response procedures are another crucial aspect of securing Active Directory. Organizations should develop an incident response plan that includes clear steps for identifying, reporting, and mitigating security incidents related to AD. This plan should encompass monitoring for unusual activities, such as unauthorized access attempts or changes to critical objects within AD. Utilizing PowerShell scripts for automation can help IT professionals streamline incident detection and response efforts, allowing for real-time alerts and rapid remediation. Regular training for staff on recognizing and responding to potential security threats can further bolster an organization's overall security readiness.

Finally, organizations must prioritize the integration of Active Directory with cloud-based solutions, such as Azure Active Directory, while maintaining security best practices. This involves configuring secure authentication protocols, such as Multi-Factor Authentication (MFA), to protect user identities in cloud environments. Regularly auditing and reviewing security configurations in both on-premises and cloud environments is essential for ensuring compliance with industry standards and regulations. By adopting a proactive approach to securing Active Directory through well-defined policies and procedures, small businesses can safeguard their networks against evolving cyber threats while ensuring operational efficiency and compliance.

Monitoring and Auditing for Security

Monitoring and auditing for security within Active Directory (AD) are critical components for small businesses and IT professionals aiming to safeguard their networks. Active Directory serves as the backbone of user management and authentication in many organizations, making it a prime target for cyber threats. By implementing robust monitoring and auditing practices, businesses can not only detect suspicious activities but also ensure compliance with industry standards and regulations. This subchapter will explore the tools and techniques available for effective security monitoring and auditing in Active Directory environments.

A comprehensive monitoring strategy begins with the establishment of baseline behaviors within the Active Directory environment. Understanding what constitutes normal activity is essential for identifying anomalies that could indicate a security breach. IT professionals should utilize PowerShell scripts to automate the collection of user login events, group policy changes, and directory modifications. By archiving these logs and analyzing them over time, organizations can detect trends and unusual patterns that warrant further investigation. Furthermore, integrating these logs with a Security Information and Event Management (SIEM) system enhances the ability to correlate events across different systems, providing a holistic view of the security landscape.

Auditing is equally important, as it provides a historical record of changes made within Active Directory. Regularly reviewing audit logs helps organizations identify unauthorized access attempts,

VICTOR P HENDERSON | ISSO-TECH ENTERPRISES™
CERTIFIED ETHICAL HACKER C|EH

ISSO-TECH PRESS™

changes to user permissions, and modifications to group memberships. PowerShell can be leveraged to generate detailed reports of these activities, enabling IT professionals to scrutinize the audit trails effectively. By configuring advanced auditing features in Active Directory, businesses can fine-tune what events are logged, ensuring that they capture the most relevant information without overwhelming their systems with excessive data.

In addition to monitoring and auditing internal activities, small businesses must also consider the security implications of integrating Active Directory with cloud environments such as Azure AD. As organizations increasingly adopt hybrid models, the need for comprehensive visibility across on-premises and cloud-based resources becomes paramount. Implementing consistent monitoring practices across these platforms ensures that security policies are enforced uniformly, reducing the risk of vulnerabilities arising from misconfigurations or overlooked permissions. Automated alerts for unusual activities such as logins from unfamiliar devices or geographic locations can help organizations respond swiftly to potential threats.

Finally, establishing a culture of security awareness is integral to the success of monitoring and auditing efforts. IT professionals and network engineers must work collaboratively to educate employees about the importance of following security best practices and recognizing potential threats. Regular training sessions and updates on new security protocols can empower all users to contribute to the organization's overall security posture. By integrating these educational efforts with automated monitoring tools and regular auditing processes, small businesses can create a resilient Active Directory environment that not only protects sensitive information but also instills confidence among stakeholders and clients alike.

ACTIVE DIRECTORY GROUP POLICY MANAGEMENT

Understanding Group Policies

Group Policies are a critical component of Active Directory (AD), serving as a powerful tool for managing user and computer settings within a network. For small businesses, IT professionals, network engineers, and system engineers, an in-depth understanding of Group Policies can significantly enhance operational efficiency and security. By defining specific configurations for users and computers, Group Policies ensure a consistent and secure environment that aligns with organizational policies and compliance requirements. This chapter aims to demystify Group Policies, providing insights into their structure, implementation, and best practices for management.

At the core of Group Policy is the Group Policy Object (GPO), which encapsulates the settings that dictate the behavior of user accounts and computer accounts within an AD environment. GPOs can be linked to Active Directory containers such as sites, domains, and organizational units (OUs), thereby allowing for granular control over policy application. Understanding the hierarchy of GPOs is essential; policies applied at a site level take precedence over those at the domain or OU level. This hierarchical structure enables IT professionals to tailor settings based on specific organizational needs while ensuring that broader policies do not conflict with localized configurations.

Implementing Group Policies effectively involves a thorough assessment of the organization's requirements and an understanding of the potential impact of each policy setting. For instance, security settings such as password policies, account lockout policies, and user rights assignments can significantly influence the security posture of an organization. Additionally, settings related to software installation, network configurations, and desktop environments are vital for enhancing user productivity while minimizing support overhead. By leveraging PowerShell, IT professionals can automate the creation, modification, and application of GPOs, streamlining the management process and reducing the likelihood of errors.

Another essential aspect of Group Policy management is troubleshooting. IT professionals must be adept at identifying and resolving issues that may arise from GPO application failures or conflicts. Common challenges include slow logon times, unexpected behavior in user environments, and discrepancies between intended and actual settings. Utilizing tools such as the Group Policy Results wizard and the Group Policy Modeling tool can help diagnose issues effectively. Furthermore, maintaining documentation on GPO changes and implementations is crucial for auditing purposes, ensuring compliance with industry standards, and facilitating disaster recovery planning.

In conclusion, mastering Group Policies is indispensable for small businesses and IT professionals focused on enhancing their Active Directory environments. By understanding the structure and application of GPOs, effectively implementing and troubleshooting them, and leveraging automation tools like PowerShell, organizations can create a resilient and efficient IT infrastructure. As businesses increasingly migrate to cloud environments and integrate solutions like Azure Active Directory, the principles of Group Policy management remain pertinent, ensuring that security and compliance are upheld across all platforms. The insights gained from this chapter will empower IT professionals to harness the full potential of Group Policies, ultimately contributing to improved operational effectiveness and security.

Creating and Managing Group Policies

Creating and managing Group Policies is a fundamental aspect of Active Directory (AD) administration that plays a critical role in the configuration and security of IT environments. For small businesses, IT professionals, network engineers, and system engineers, understanding how to effectively implement and manage Group Policies can lead to substantial improvements in efficiency and security. Group Policies are a powerful tool that allows for the centralized management of user and computer settings across the network, ensuring that all devices adhere to the organization's security and operational standards.

The process begins with defining the scope of the Group Policies you wish to implement. This involves identifying the Organizational Units (OUs) that will receive specific policies, which can range from password complexity requirements to software installation settings. For small businesses, it is essential to tailor these policies according to the unique needs of the organization while considering the potential impact on user productivity. Properly structuring OUs can simplify management and ensure that policies are applied consistently across related groups of users and computers.

Once the scope is defined, the creation of Group Policies can be approached through the Group Policy Management Console (GPMC). This interface provides a user-friendly means to create, edit, and link Group Policies to the appropriate OUs. For IT professionals, leveraging PowerShell can automate many of these tasks, enabling the rapid deployment of policies across multiple

OUs or even entire domains. Automating these processes not only saves time but also reduces the risk of human error during policy creation and management, which is crucial in maintaining security compliance.

Managing Group Policies also requires ongoing attention to ensure they remain relevant and effective. Regular reviews of existing policies can help identify any that are outdated or no longer serve the organization's needs. Additionally, leveraging tools such as Resultant Set of Policy (RSoP) and Group Policy Modeling can assist in troubleshooting potential issues before they affect users. For network and system engineers, understanding how to utilize these tools is vital for maintaining a stable and secure Active Directory environment.

Finally, integrating Group Policy management with other Active Directory tasks, such as auditing and compliance, enhances overall security posture. Regular audits of Group Policies can help verify that they align with best practices and regulatory requirements. Furthermore, as organizations increasingly adopt cloud environments, the integration of Group Policies with Azure Active Directory becomes critical. This ensures that policies apply consistently across on-premises and cloud resources, providing a seamless user experience while maintaining robust security controls. By mastering Group Policy management, IT professionals can significantly enhance their organization's operational efficiency and security framework.

Troubleshooting Group Policy Issues

Group Policy is a powerful tool in Active Directory that allows IT professionals to manage users and computers within a network efficiently. However, issues can arise that disrupt the intended policy application, leading to inconsistent configurations and user experiences. For small businesses and IT professionals, understanding how to troubleshoot these issues is crucial for maintaining an efficient and secure environment. This subchapter will explore common problems encountered with Group Policy and provide actionable strategies for resolution, ensuring that network engineers and system engineers can keep their Active Directory environments running smoothly.

One of the first steps in troubleshooting Group Policy issues is to verify the application of the policies. IT professionals should utilize the Resultant Set of Policy (RSoP) tool, which helps to determine what policies are being applied to a specific user or computer. By running the RSoP in both logging and planning modes, administrators can identify whether the expected policies are being enforced and trace any discrepancies. Additionally, understanding the order of Group Policy processing—Local, Site, Domain, and Organizational Unit (OU)—is essential. Misconfigurations or conflicts in this hierarchy can lead to unexpected behavior, and careful examination of the Group Policy Objects (GPOs) in use is necessary.

Another common issue involves the scope of the GPO. Often, policies may not be applying due to incorrect security filtering or WMI filtering settings. Administrators should ensure that the intended user or computer accounts are included in the security filtering settings and that the WMI filters are correctly configured to match the desired conditions. Furthermore, reviewing the delegation settings for the GPO is critical, as improper permissions can prevent users from receiving the policies. Leveraging PowerShell commands can streamline the process of checking these configurations, allowing for rapid identification and resolution of issues.

Network connectivity problems can also impede the application of Group Policies. IT professionals should verify that affected computers are properly connected to the network and can communicate with domain controllers. Using tools such as Ping and nslookup can help diagnose connectivity issues, while the Group Policy Results Wizard can provide insights into the last successful application of policies. Additionally, examining the event logs on both the client and server sides can reveal underlying errors that may be contributing to the problem. Regularly monitoring network health and ensuring that DNS settings are properly configured can help mitigate these issues proactively.

Finally, it is essential to incorporate best practices for ongoing management and monitoring of Group Policies. Regular audits of GPOs can help identify outdated or conflicting policies that may cause issues in the future. Implementing a systematic approach to change management, including documentation and version control for GPO modifications, can ensure that all changes are tracked and can be reverted if necessary. Furthermore, leveraging automation tools in PowerShell can enhance efficiency in both troubleshooting and managing Group Policy, empowering IT professionals to maintain a robust and compliant Active Directory environment. By

© **MASTERING ACTIVE DIRECTORY**

@ISSO.TECH.ENTERPRISES

following these strategies, small businesses and IT professionals can ensure that their Group Policy implementations support their operational goals effectively.

AUDITING AND COMPLIANCE IN ACTIVE DIRECTORY

Understanding Auditing Requirements

Understanding auditing requirements is a crucial aspect for small businesses and IT professionals managing Active Directory (AD) environments. As organizations increasingly rely on AD for user authentication and resource management, the need for robust auditing practices becomes paramount. Auditing provides a comprehensive framework for monitoring changes within the directory, ensuring compliance with regulatory standards, and enhancing overall security posture. This subchapter delves into the essential auditing requirements that IT professionals must consider to effectively protect their Active Directory infrastructure.

To begin with, it is essential to identify the key components of Active Directory that require auditing. These components include user account management, group membership changes, and modifications to Group Policy Objects (GPOs). Each of these areas represents a potential risk if not properly monitored. For instance, unauthorized changes to user accounts can lead to security breaches, while modifications to GPOs can inadvertently affect system configurations across the network. Therefore, establishing a clear understanding of what needs to be audited is the first step toward creating a comprehensive auditing strategy.

Next, organizations must familiarize themselves with the various auditing standards and compliance requirements relevant to their industry. Many sectors, including finance and healthcare, are subject to strict regulations that mandate specific auditing practices. The Health Insurance Portability and Accountability Act

@ISSO.TECH.ENTERPRISES

(HIPAA) and the Payment Card Industry Data Security Standard (PCI DSS) are two examples of regulations that necessitate thorough auditing of AD environments. By aligning their auditing practices with these standards, IT professionals can ensure that their organizations not only meet legal obligations but also foster a culture of accountability and transparency.

Implementing effective auditing practices involves leveraging PowerShell, a powerful scripting language that can automate many aspects of AD management. PowerShell enables IT professionals to create scripts that generate comprehensive reports on user activity, changes to security groups, and modifications to GPOs. By automating the auditing process, organizations can significantly reduce the time and effort required to monitor their AD environments while simultaneously increasing accuracy and consistency in reporting. This automation is particularly beneficial for small businesses that may lack the resources for extensive manual auditing processes.

Finally, organizations must regularly review and update their auditing policies and practices to adapt to evolving threats and compliance requirements. This ongoing assessment is vital in ensuring that auditing mechanisms remain effective in capturing relevant data and providing actionable insights. IT professionals should establish a routine for evaluating their auditing processes, incorporating feedback from audits into their policies, and staying informed about changes in regulatory landscapes. By fostering a proactive approach to auditing, small businesses can better

VICTOR P HENDERSON | ISSO-TECH ENTERPRISES™
CERTIFIED ETHICAL HACKER C|EH

ISSO-TECH PRESS™

safeguard their Active Directory environments and enhance their overall security posture.

Implementing Auditing Solutions

Implementing effective auditing solutions in Active Directory (AD) is essential for maintaining security and ensuring compliance, especially for small businesses and IT professionals tasked with managing networks. As organizations increasingly rely on Active Directory to authenticate users and manage resources, the need for robust auditing measures becomes paramount. This subchapter delves into the strategies and tools necessary to implement effective auditing solutions, enabling IT professionals, network engineers, and system engineers to enhance their Active Directory environments.

To begin, it is critical to define the objectives of auditing within Active Directory. Auditing serves not only as a tool for compliance but also as a proactive measure to identify potential security incidents before they escalate. By establishing clear goals—such as monitoring user access, tracking changes to group policies, and identifying unauthorized modifications—organizations can tailor their auditing solutions to meet specific security needs. A well-structured auditing strategy fosters accountability and transparency, ensuring that all actions within the AD environment are traceable.

Next, leveraging PowerShell for automating auditing tasks can significantly boost efficiency. PowerShell provides a powerful framework for scripting and automating the collection of audit logs, allowing IT professionals to streamline the monitoring process. By creating scripts that routinely check for changes in user permissions, group memberships, and other critical attributes, organizations can generate reports that provide insights into the state of their Active Directory. This automation not only saves time but also reduces the risk of human error, which is a common pitfall in manual auditing processes.

Integrating auditing solutions with existing security policies and compliance frameworks is another vital aspect of implementation. Small businesses must ensure that their auditing practices align with regulatory requirements such as GDPR or HIPAA. This alignment can be achieved by configuring audit policies that reflect the necessary compliance standards and ensuring that logs are stored securely and retained for the required duration. Moreover, the integration of auditing with other security measures, such as intrusion detection systems, enhances the overall security posture and provides a comprehensive view of the organization's security landscape.

Finally, ongoing evaluation and adaptation of auditing solutions are essential to keep pace with evolving threats and organizational changes. Regularly reviewing audit logs and assessing the effectiveness of existing policies can help identify gaps and areas for improvement. Additionally, as businesses transition to cloud environments or integrate with platforms like Azure AD, it becomes increasingly important to adapt auditing strategies accordingly. Continuous education and training for IT professionals in emerging trends and best practices in Active Directory auditing will empower them to respond effectively to new challenges, ensuring that their organizations remain secure and compliant.

@ISSO.TECH.ENTERPRISES

By implementing robust auditing solutions within Active Directory, small businesses and IT professionals can significantly enhance their security posture while ensuring compliance with industry standards. Through the use of automation, alignment with security policies, and ongoing evaluation, organizations can establish a sustainable approach to auditing that not only meets current needs but also adapts to future challenges. As the landscape of IT continues to evolve, mastering the intricacies of Active Directory auditing will be a critical competency for professionals dedicated to safeguarding their organizations.

Compliance Frameworks and Best Practices

In the realm of Active Directory (AD) management, particularly for small businesses and IT professionals, establishing a robust compliance framework is crucial for ensuring security and operational efficiency. Compliance frameworks provide structured methodologies that help organizations adhere to regulatory requirements, industry standards, and best practices while managing their Active Directory environments. These frameworks not only safeguard sensitive information but also streamline processes, making it essential for network and system engineers to integrate them into their daily operations.

One of the foundational elements of a compliance framework is the identification and implementation of security best practices tailored for Active Directory. These practices include regular auditing of user accounts and permissions, password policies that enforce complexity and expiration, and the principle of least privilege, which ensures that users have only the access necessary for their roles. By adhering to these best practices, organizations can mitigate risks associated with unauthorized access and data breaches, thereby strengthening their overall security posture. Furthermore, documenting these practices is vital, as it provides a reference point for training new IT staff and for audits that may arise.

In addition to security best practices, organizations must also consider compliance with various regulatory standards such as GDPR, HIPAA, or PCI-DSS, depending on their industry. These regulations often have specific requirements concerning data

@ISSO.TECH.ENTERPRISES

protection, user privacy, and incident reporting. Integrating compliance checks into Active Directory management processes can help small businesses ensure that they meet these obligations. Automated tools and scripts developed using PowerShell can facilitate regular compliance assessments, generating reports that highlight areas needing attention, and ensuring that the organization remains aligned with regulatory expectations.

Moreover, with the increasing adoption of cloud environments, particularly Azure Active Directory, it is imperative for IT professionals to adapt their compliance frameworks accordingly. Cloud integration introduces new challenges, such as data sovereignty and external access management, which must be addressed within the compliance structure. By leveraging PowerShell, IT teams can automate the synchronization of on-premises Active Directory with Azure AD, ensuring consistent enforcement of compliance policies across both platforms. This seamless integration not only enhances security but also improves operational efficiency by reducing manual intervention.

Lastly, continuous monitoring and improvement are integral to any compliance framework. Organizations should establish a regular review cycle to assess their compliance posture and update their practices as needed. This involves analyzing audit logs, tracking changes to Active Directory objects, and conducting periodic security assessments. By embracing a culture of compliance and ongoing improvement, small businesses can not only protect their assets but also position themselves as reliable partners in an increasingly competitive market. Through diligent adherence to

ISSO-TECH PRESS™

compliance frameworks and best practices, IT professionals can ensure that their Active Directory environments are secure, efficient, and aligned with industry standards.

ISSO-TECH

VICTOR P HENDERSON | ISSO-TECH ENTERPRISES™
CERTIFIED ETHICAL HACKER C|EH

ISSO-TECH PRESS™

CHAPTER 07
ADVANCED SERVICES

CHAPTER 7: ADVANCED SERVICES
SERVICE DEPLOYMENTS

Active Directory Federation Services (AD FS)

Active Directory Federation Services (AD FS) is a Windows Server role that provides a single sign-on (SSO) solution for authenticating users across trusted environments. AD FS allows users to access multiple applications with a single set of credentials, simplifying the user experience and enhancing security. Here's an overview of AD FS and its key features:

1. Federation Trust:

- AD FS establishes trust relationships (federation trusts) with external identity providers (IdPs) or federation partners.
- This trust allows users from one organization to access resources in another organization without the need for separate credentials.

2. Claims-based Authentication:

- AD FS uses claims-based authentication to verify a user's identity based on a set of claims (attributes) provided by the user or IdP.
- Claims include information such as user ID, email address, group membership, and role.

3. Single Sign-On (SSO):

- AD FS enables SSO, allowing users to access multiple applications or services with a single set of credentials.
- Once authenticated, users can access resources in the federated environment without having to re-enter their credentials.

VICTOR P HENDERSON | ISSO-TECH ENTERPRISES™
CERTIFIED ETHICAL HACKER C|EH

ISSO-TECH PRESS™

4. Web Application Proxy:

- AD FS can be deployed with the Web Application Proxy role to provide secure remote access to web applications.
- The Web Application Proxy acts as a reverse proxy, protecting internal web applications from external access.

5. Multifactor Authentication (MFA):

- AD FS supports multifactor authentication, allowing organizations to add an extra layer of security to the authentication process.
- MFA can be configured to require users to provide additional verification, such as a phone call, text message, or biometric scan.

6. Authorization Policies:

- AD FS allows administrators to define authorization policies based on user attributes, such as group membership or user location.
- These policies can control access to resources based on specific criteria.

7. Integration with Active Directory:

- AD FS integrates with Active Directory to authenticate users and retrieve user attributes.
- This integration allows organizations to leverage their existing Active Directory infrastructure for authentication.

8. Logging and Auditing:

- AD FS provides logging and auditing capabilities to track authentication events and monitor the health of the AD FS infrastructure.
- Administrators can review logs to identify security issues or troubleshoot authentication problems.

@ISSO.TECH.ENTERPRISES

AD FS provides a secure and flexible authentication solution for organizations that need to enable SSO across trusted environments. By leveraging AD FS, organizations can enhance security, improve user experience, and streamline access to resources.

- Active Directory Certificate Services (AD CS)
Active Directory Certificate Services (AD CS) is a Windows Server role that provides customizable services for issuing and managing public key infrastructure (PKI) certificates. AD CS allows organizations to create their own certification authority (CA) and issue certificates for secure communication within their environment. Here's an overview of AD CS and its key features:

1. Certificate Authority (CA):
- AD CS allows you to deploy one or more CAs to issue certificates to users, computers, and services.
- CAs can be standalone or enterprise CAs, with enterprise CAs integrating with Active Directory for simplified management.

2. Certificate Templates:
- AD CS provides customizable certificate templates that define the format and content of certificates issued by the CA.
- Certificate templates can be configured to meet specific security and operational requirements, such as key usage, subject name, and validity period.

3. Certificate Enrollment:
- AD CS supports various methods for users and devices to enroll for certificates, including:
- Manual enrollment through the Certificate MMC snap-in.

- Automatic enrollment using Group Policy or certificate autoenrollment.
- Web enrollment through a web interface provided by the CA.

4. Certificate Revocation:

- AD CS supports certificate revocation, allowing you to revoke certificates that are no longer valid or compromised.
- Revoked certificates are added to a Certificate Revocation List (CRL) or published to an Online Certificate Status Protocol (OCSP) responder for validation.

5. Key Archival and Recovery:

- AD CS supports key archival and recovery, allowing organizations to securely archive private keys for recovery purposes.
- Archival keys are stored in a secure location and can be recovered if a user's private key is lost or compromised.

6. Smart Card Authentication:

- AD CS can be used to issue smart card certificates for secure authentication to network resources.
- Smart card authentication provides strong, two-factor authentication using a smart card and a PIN.

7. Code Signing and Secure Email:

- AD CS can issue certificates for code signing to ensure the integrity and authenticity of software applications.
- It can also issue certificates for secure email (S/MIME) to encrypt and digitally sign email messages.

8. Integration with Active Directory:

- AD CS integrates with Active Directory to simplify certificate management and ensure that certificates are issued only to authorized users and devices.
- AD CS can use Active Directory information, such as user attributes and group membership, to populate certificate fields and enforce certificate issuance policies.

AD CS provides a comprehensive PKI solution for organizations that need to secure their network communications, authenticate users and devices, and ensure the integrity and confidentiality of their data. By deploying AD CS, organizations can establish a trusted and secure environment for their network resources.

- Active Directory Lightweight Directory Services (AD LDS)
Active Directory Lightweight Directory Services (AD LDS), formerly known as Active Directory Application Mode (ADAM), is a Lightweight Directory Access Protocol (LDAP) directory service from Microsoft. It provides a data store and directory service for applications that do not require the full features of Active Directory Domain Services (AD DS). Here's an overview of AD LDS and its key features:

1. Stand-Alone Directory Service:

- AD LDS operates as a stand-alone directory service and does not require a full Active Directory domain infrastructure.
- It can be used to store application-specific data, such as user accounts, without the need for a complete domain environment.

2. Flexible Schema:

- AD LDS allows you to define a custom schema to store and manage data specific to your application.
- You can extend the schema to include custom object classes and attributes tailored to your application's needs.

3. LDAP Protocol Support:

- AD LDS supports the LDAP protocol, allowing applications to access and manage directory data using standard LDAP operations.
- It also supports LDAPS (LDAP over SSL/TLS) for secure communication.

4. Authentication and Authorization:

- AD LDS can be used for authentication and authorization, allowing applications to validate user credentials and control access to resources.
- It supports simple authentication as well as more advanced mechanisms such as Kerberos and NTLM.

5. Replication:

- AD LDS supports replication of directory data between instances, allowing you to deploy multiple instances for redundancy and scalability.
- Replication can be configured to replicate data between instances on the same server or across different servers.

6. Integration with AD DS:

- AD LDS can be integrated with AD DS to share schema and configuration information.
- This integration allows you to use existing AD DS tools and infrastructure to manage AD LDS instances.

@ISSO.TECH.ENTERPRISES

7. Application Partitioning:

- AD LDS supports partitioning of directory data into application partitions, allowing you to organize data based on application requirements.
- Each application partition can have its own security settings and replication scope.

8. Lightweight Installation:

- AD LDS has a lightweight installation footprint compared to AD DS, making it suitable for use in environments where resource constraints are a concern.

AD LDS is well-suited for applications that require a lightweight directory service with a flexible schema, support for LDAP, and authentication and authorization capabilities. It allows developers to build applications that leverage directory services without the complexity of a full AD DS deployment.

ISSO-TECH PRESS™

ACTIVE DIRECTORY FOR CLOUD ENVIRONMENTS

Integrating Active Directory with Cloud Services

Integrating Active Directory (AD) with cloud services is pivotal for small businesses looking to leverage the scalability and flexibility of cloud computing while maintaining robust security and management practices. As organizations increasingly migrate to cloud environments, the integration of on-premises Active Directory with cloud services such as Azure Active Directory (Azure AD) becomes essential. This integration not only streamlines user management but also enhances security, allowing businesses to utilize familiar Active Directory features in a cloud context. By employing PowerShell automation, IT professionals can efficiently manage these integrations, ensuring that administrative tasks are performed with minimal overhead.

The first step in integrating Active Directory with cloud services is establishing a secure connection between on-premises AD and Azure AD. This typically involves using Azure AD Connect, a tool designed to synchronize on-premises directories with Azure AD. By configuring Azure AD Connect, businesses can ensure that user credentials, group memberships, and other relevant data are replicated in the cloud environment. This synchronization allows users to maintain a single identity across both environments, simplifying the user experience and reducing the administrative burden associated with managing multiple identities. PowerShell scripts can be employed to automate the configuration and ongoing management of Azure AD Connect, thus improving efficiency and reducing the potential for human error.

@ISSO.TECH.ENTERPRISES

Security best practices play a critical role in the integration process. Implementing Multi-Factor Authentication (MFA) within Azure AD is one of the foremost recommendations to enhance security. By requiring a second form of verification, MFA mitigates the risk of unauthorized access, especially in environments where remote work is prevalent. Additionally, it is paramount to regularly audit and monitor both Active Directory and Azure AD environments for compliance with security policies. PowerShell can be utilized to automate auditing tasks, generating reports on user access patterns, group memberships, and other critical security metrics. This practice not only helps in identifying potential vulnerabilities but also assists in ensuring compliance with relevant regulations.

Moreover, the management of Group Policies becomes increasingly complex in a hybrid environment. IT professionals must ensure that policies applied in on-premises AD are adequately reflected in Azure AD. The integration allows for the application of cloud-based policies, which can be managed through Microsoft Endpoint Manager or similar tools. Utilizing PowerShell, administrators can create scripts to manage and automate the deployment of Group Policies across both environments, ensuring consistency and compliance. This not only saves time but also reduces the risk of misconfiguration, which can lead to security vulnerabilities.

In conclusion, integrating Active Directory with cloud services is not merely a technical necessity but a strategic imperative for small businesses aiming to harness the full potential of modern IT solutions. By utilizing tools such as Azure AD Connect and leveraging PowerShell for automation, IT professionals can effectively manage user identities and security policies across hybrid environments. The benefits of this integration extend beyond operational efficiency; they also encompass enhanced security, streamlined compliance, and improved overall management of IT resources. As businesses continue to evolve in the digital landscape, mastering these integration strategies will be essential for maintaining a competitive edge and ensuring robust, secure operations.

@ISSO.TECH.ENTERPRISES

Managing Hybrid Environments

Managing hybrid environments, which combine on-premises Active Directory (AD) with cloud-based solutions like Azure Active Directory (Azure AD), presents unique challenges and opportunities for IT professionals. As small businesses increasingly adopt a hybrid model to leverage the benefits of both local and cloud infrastructures, understanding the intricacies of managing these environments becomes indispensable. This subchapter will explore best practices for integrating and securing hybrid AD setups, ensuring seamless operations, and enhancing overall efficiency.

The first step in managing a hybrid environment is establishing a robust integration strategy between on-premises AD and Azure AD. This involves deploying Azure AD Connect, a tool that synchronizes identities across both platforms, allowing users to leverage the same credentials when accessing resources in either environment. Properly configuring Azure AD Connect can help mitigate potential authentication issues, enhance user experience, and simplify management. Additionally, IT professionals should regularly review synchronization settings to accommodate changes in organizational structure or technology, ensuring that all user identities are current and accurately represented in both environments.

Security is paramount in hybrid environments, necessitating a comprehensive approach to Active Directory security best practices. This includes implementing Multi-Factor Authentication (MFA) for users accessing cloud resources, which significantly reduces the risk of unauthorized access. Regularly auditing user permissions and group memberships is also critical to maintaining a secure environment. By leveraging PowerShell scripts, IT professionals can automate the auditing process, streamlining the identification of any potential security vulnerabilities related to user access and permissions across both on-premises and cloud infrastructures.

Effective Group Policy Management is another cornerstone of managing hybrid environments. Group Policies not only govern user settings and security configurations within the on-premises AD but can also be extended to manage devices and users in Azure AD. Understanding the differences in policy application between environments is crucial, as improper configurations can lead to conflicts or unintended consequences. Utilizing PowerShell to automate the deployment and management of Group Policies can save valuable time and reduce errors, allowing IT professionals to focus on higher-level strategic initiatives.

Finally, troubleshooting Active Directory issues in a hybrid context requires a thorough understanding of both environments. Professionals must be adept at using diagnostic tools and PowerShell cmdlets to identify and resolve problems that may arise from synchronization errors, authentication failures, or policy application discrepancies. Establishing a systematic approach to troubleshooting—documenting issues, resolutions, and lessons learned—can enhance overall operational efficiency. By integrating these practices, small businesses can ensure that their hybrid environments function optimally, supporting their growth and technological advancements while maintaining a strong security posture.

Security Considerations in Cloud Integration

In the contemporary landscape of IT, the integration of cloud services with Active Directory (AD) represents a significant advancement, particularly for small businesses and IT professionals. However, this integration comes with a spectrum of security considerations that must be diligently addressed. As organizations increasingly migrate their operations to the cloud, understanding the security implications of this shift is paramount to safeguarding sensitive data and maintaining compliance with regulatory requirements. This subchapter will explore essential security practices that should be implemented during cloud integration, focusing on the unique challenges faced by small businesses and IT professionals.

One of the primary concerns when integrating Active Directory with cloud environments is the potential exposure of sensitive information. Small businesses often lack the extensive resources available to larger organizations, making them attractive targets for cybercriminals. Therefore, it is critical to adopt robust security measures, such as multi-factor authentication (MFA) and strong password policies, to enhance the security posture of Active Directory. Implementing MFA can significantly reduce the risk of unauthorized access, as it requires users to provide multiple forms of verification before gaining access to cloud resources. Additionally, enforcing complex password requirements can mitigate the risk of credential theft, a common vector for attacks on cloud-integrated environments.

Another crucial area for consideration is the security of data in transit and at rest. When integrating AD with cloud platforms like Azure AD, data flows between on-premises infrastructure and the cloud, potentially exposing it to interception during transmission. To combat this, organizations should employ encryption protocols such as TLS/SSL for data in transit, ensuring that sensitive information remains secure as it travels across networks. Furthermore, data stored in the cloud should be encrypted at rest, providing an additional layer of protection against unauthorized access. These measures not only fortify security but also help organizations comply with data protection regulations that mandate the safeguarding of personal and sensitive information.

Access control is a foundational aspect of security that must be meticulously managed during cloud integration. IT professionals must implement least privilege access principles, ensuring that users are granted only the permissions necessary to perform their job functions. This minimizes the risk of internal threats and accidental data exposure. Additionally, it is essential to regularly review and audit user permissions to identify and revoke access that is no longer needed. By maintaining a rigorous access control framework, organizations can better defend against both external and internal security breaches, providing a secure environment for their cloud-integrated Active Directory.

Lastly, the importance of continuous monitoring and incident response cannot be overstated. Cloud environments are dynamic, and security threats are constantly evolving. Small businesses must establish a proactive monitoring system that tracks user activities, detects anomalies, and alerts IT personnel to potential security incidents. Coupled with an effective incident response plan, this approach enables organizations to swiftly address security breaches, minimizing damage and restoring normal operations efficiently. Regular training and awareness programs for employees can further enhance security by fostering a culture of vigilance and accountability.

In conclusion, the integration of Active Directory with cloud services offers substantial benefits for small businesses, but it is accompanied by critical security considerations that cannot be overlooked. By implementing strong authentication measures, ensuring data encryption, enforcing strict access controls, and maintaining robust monitoring practices, organizations can create a secure environment that leverages the advantages of cloud technology while protecting their most valuable assets. Understanding and addressing these security challenges will empower IT professionals and network engineers to effectively manage Active Directory in the cloud, ultimately contributing to the overall resilience and success of their organizations.

@ISSO.TECH.ENTERPRISES

ISSO-TECH

VICTOR P HENDERSON | ISSO-TECH ENTERPRISES™
CERTIFIED ETHICAL HACKER C|EH

ISSO-TECH PRESS™

229.320.151.8

CHAPTER 08
DATA RECOVERY

CHAPTER 8 | DISASTER RECOVERY
DATA BACKUP & RECOVERY

Backup strategies for Active Directory

Implementing a robust backup strategy for Active Directory (AD) is critical to ensure that you can recover from accidental deletions, hardware failures, or other disasters that may result in data loss. Here are key elements to consider when planning your AD backup strategy:

1. Regular Backups:

- Perform regular backups of the Active Directory database (NTDS.dit) and system state, which includes critical system files and the registry.
- Schedule backups to run daily or as frequently as needed based on your organization's requirements.

2. Backup Storage:

- Store backups in a secure location, preferably on a separate server or storage device from the production AD environment.
- Consider using offsite or cloud storage for additional protection against on-premises disasters.

3. Backup Retention:

- Define a backup retention policy to determine how long backup copies should be retained.
- Consider regulatory requirements and best practices when setting retention periods.

4. Testing Backups:

- Regularly test your backup and restore procedures to ensure they work as expected.
- Test restores to a separate environment to verify that backups are valid and can be restored successfully.

5. Backup and Restore Procedures:

- Document backup and restore procedures, including step-by-step instructions for performing backups and recoveries.
- Ensure that key personnel are trained on these procedures and can perform them effectively.

6. Monitoring and Alerts:

- Implement monitoring to alert you of backup failures or other issues that may impact the integrity of your backups.
- Regularly review backup logs and alerts to ensure that backups are running as scheduled.

7. Versioning and Incremental Backups:

- Consider using versioning or incremental backups to minimize backup storage requirements and speed up backup processes.
- These methods only backup changes made since the last backup, reducing the amount of data that needs to be backed up.

8. Backup Software:

- Use reputable backup software that supports Active Directory backups and offers features such as encryption, compression, and scheduling.
- Ensure that the backup software is compatible with your AD environment and meets your organization's requirements.

@ISSO.TECH.ENTERPRISES

By implementing a comprehensive backup strategy for Active Directory, you can minimize the risk of data loss and ensure that your organization can quickly recover from disasters or other events that may impact AD.
- Restoring Active Directory

Restoring Active Directory (AD) is a critical process that requires careful planning and execution to ensure the recovery of your AD environment. Here's a general outline of the steps involved in restoring AD from backup:

1. Prepare for the Restore:
- Ensure that you have a recent backup of the Active Directory database (NTDS.dit) and system state.
- Verify that the backup is valid and can be restored successfully.

2. Start the Domain Controller in Directory Services Restore Mode (DSRM):
- Restart the domain controller and press F8 before Windows starts to access the advanced boot options.
- Select "Directory Services Restore Mode" from the boot options menu.

3. Perform the Restore:
- Use the backup software to restore the Active Directory database (NTDS.dit) and system state.
- Follow the instructions provided by the backup software to complete the restore process.

4. Restart the Domain Controller:
- After the restore process is complete, restart the domain controller normally.
- The domain controller will start in normal mode and should be operational.

5. Verify the Restore:
- Log in to the domain controller and verify that AD is functioning correctly.
- Check event logs and perform basic tests to ensure that AD is working as expected.

6. Perform Additional Steps (if needed):
- Depending on the nature of the restore, you may need to perform additional steps, such as seizing FSMO roles or cleaning up metadata for failed domain controllers.

7. Monitor the Domain Controller:
- Monitor the restored domain controller for any issues or errors.
- Check replication status and ensure that the domain controller is properly communicating with other domain controllers in the environment.

8. Update Documentation:
- Update your backup and restore documentation to reflect the restore process and any changes made during the restore.
It's important to test your backup and restore procedures regularly to ensure that they work as expected. Additionally, consider using backup software that provides automated and reliable backup and restore capabilities for Active Directory.
- Planning for disaster recovery

@ISSO.TECH.ENTERPRISES

Planning for disaster recovery (DR) is crucial to ensure business continuity in the event of a disaster or unexpected event. Here are key steps to consider when planning for DR for Active Directory (AD):

1. Risk Assessment:
- Identify potential risks and threats that could impact your AD environment, such as hardware failure, natural disasters, cyberattacks, or human error.

2. Business Impact Analysis (BIA):
- Conduct a BIA to determine the potential impact of an AD failure on your organization's operations, finances, and reputation.
- Use the BIA to prioritize recovery efforts and allocate resources effectively.

3. Define Recovery Objectives:
- Define recovery time objectives (RTOs) and recovery point objectives (RPOs) for AD.
- RTO is the maximum acceptable downtime for AD services, while RPO is the maximum amount of data loss acceptable.

4. Backup Strategy:
- Implement a robust backup strategy for AD, including regular backups of the AD database (NTDS.dit) and system state.
- Consider using incremental backups and offsite storage for added protection.

5. Replication:
- Implement AD replication between domain controllers to ensure redundancy and availability.

- Use multiple domain controllers in different locations to mitigate the risk of a single point of failure.

6. High Availability:
- Consider implementing high availability solutions for AD, such as clustering or virtualization, to ensure continuous availability of AD services.

7. Testing and Training:
- Regularly test your DR plan to ensure that it works as expected.
- Train IT staff on their roles and responsibilities during a DR event.

8. Documentation:
- Maintain detailed documentation of your DR plan, including procedures for backup, recovery, and failover.
- Update the documentation regularly to reflect changes in your AD environment.

9. Communication Plan:
- Develop a communication plan to keep stakeholders informed during a DR event.
- Ensure that contact information for key personnel and vendors is up to date.

@ISSO.TECH.ENTERPRISES

10. Review and Update:
- Regularly review and update your DR plan to reflect changes in your AD environment, technology, and business requirements.
- Conduct periodic audits and assessments to ensure that your DR plan remains effective.
By following these steps, you can develop a comprehensive DR plan for Active Directory that helps ensure the availability and integrity of your AD environment in the event of a disaster.

ACTIVE DIRECTORY DISASTER RECOVERY PLANNING

Importance of Disaster Recovery

Disaster recovery is a critical component for any organization, and its significance cannot be overstated, particularly for small businesses that rely heavily on their IT infrastructure. In the realm of Active Directory (AD), effective disaster recovery planning ensures that organizations can swiftly restore their systems and services following an unexpected disruption. This is especially pertinent given the increasing number of cyber threats and natural disasters that can compromise IT operations. By implementing robust disaster recovery strategies, small businesses can safeguard their data, maintain operational continuity, and protect their reputation in the marketplace.

A well-structured disaster recovery plan for Active Directory encompasses not only the restoration of user accounts and permissions but also the recovery of policies, group settings, and other critical configurations. Small businesses are often vulnerable due to limited resources, making it essential to identify and prioritize the most crucial elements of their Active Directory environment. By automating recovery processes using PowerShell, IT professionals can significantly reduce the time and effort required to restore services, ensuring that businesses can return to normal operations with minimal downtime.

Moreover, disaster recovery is intrinsically linked to security best practices in Active Directory. A comprehensive recovery plan must involve regular backups of AD data and configurations, including Group Policies and Domain Controllers. These backups serve as a safety net, allowing organizations to recover from data loss incidents, whether due to accidental deletions, malicious attacks, or system failures. Implementing automated scripts in PowerShell for routine backups and recovery can enhance the reliability and efficiency of these processes, empowering IT professionals to focus on more strategic initiatives.

The integration of Active Directory with cloud environments further underscores the importance of disaster recovery. As businesses increasingly adopt hybrid models, their reliance on cloud services elevates the need for a cohesive recovery strategy that encompasses both on-premises and cloud-based resources. IT professionals must ensure that their disaster recovery plans are adaptable to these changes, allowing for seamless restoration of services across multiple platforms. Utilizing PowerShell can facilitate the management of these environments, enabling quick adaptations to recovery plans as business needs evolve.

Finally, a robust disaster recovery framework not only addresses technological aspects but also encompasses auditing and compliance requirements. Regulatory bodies often mandate stringent data protection measures, and having a documented disaster recovery plan can assist small businesses in demonstrating compliance. By regularly testing and updating recovery procedures, organizations can ensure they are prepared to meet both internal and external standards. This proactive approach not only enhances operational resilience but also fosters a culture of accountability and preparedness within the organization, ultimately contributing to long-term success.

Developing a Disaster Recovery Plan

Developing a disaster recovery plan is a crucial step for small businesses and IT professionals who aim to safeguard their Active Directory (AD) environments. In the face of unexpected disruptions—ranging from natural disasters to cyberattacks—having a structured plan ensures that your organization can quickly resume operations and minimize downtime. This section will outline the essential components of creating a comprehensive disaster recovery plan tailored specifically for Active Directory, empowering IT professionals, network engineers, and system engineers to effectively manage risks associated with their AD systems.

The first step in developing a disaster recovery plan is to conduct a thorough risk assessment. This involves identifying potential threats to your Active Directory infrastructure, such as hardware failures, software bugs, and external attacks. By evaluating the likelihood and impact of these risks, organizations can prioritize their recovery efforts. Small businesses often operate with limited resources, making it imperative to focus on the most critical components of their AD environment. A detailed understanding of what could go wrong enables IT teams to allocate resources effectively and plan for contingencies that align with their operational needs.

Once the risks have been identified, the next phase is to establish recovery objectives. This includes defining the Recovery Time Objective (RTO) and Recovery Point Objective (RPO) for your Active Directory services. The RTO specifies how quickly you need to restore services after a disruption, while the RPO indicates the maximum amount of data loss you can tolerate. Setting these objectives is essential for developing a realistic recovery strategy, as they inform the selection of tools and processes needed for recovery. IT professionals must ensure that these objectives align with the overall business continuity goals of their organization.

Next, organizations should document their recovery procedures in a clear and accessible manner. This documentation serves as a roadmap for IT teams during a disaster, detailing step-by-step instructions on how to restore Active Directory services. It should include information on backup procedures, restoration processes, and roles and responsibilities for team members involved in the recovery efforts. Additionally, incorporating automated scripts using PowerShell can enhance the efficiency of these procedures, allowing for quicker recovery times and reducing the potential for human error.

Finally, regular testing and updates of the disaster recovery plan are essential to ensure its effectiveness. Conducting periodic drills helps confirm that all team members are familiar with their roles and that the recovery procedures work as intended. Moreover, as changes occur in your Active Directory environment—such as new applications, updated systems, or changes in business processes—it's vital to revisit and revise the disaster recovery plan accordingly. By fostering a culture of preparedness and continuous improvement, small businesses and IT professionals can enhance their resilience against disruptions, ensuring that their Active Directory systems remain robust and reliable.

Testing and Maintaining Recovery Solutions

Testing and maintaining recovery solutions for Active Directory (AD) is critical for ensuring business continuity and minimizing downtime in the event of system failures or security incidents. For small businesses and IT professionals, the implications of an untested or improperly maintained recovery solution can be severe, potentially leading to data loss and significant operational disruptions. Therefore, establishing a robust testing and maintenance protocol is essential for any organization leveraging Active Directory, especially in environments where data integrity and security are paramount.

The first step in ensuring effective recovery solutions is to conduct regular testing of backup processes. This involves not only verifying that backups are being created as scheduled but also ensuring that the backups are complete and free from corruption. IT professionals should implement automated scripts using PowerShell to facilitate regular checks of backup integrity. These scripts can be scheduled to run at intervals that suit the organization's operational needs, providing timely notifications in the event of any failures. By proactively testing recovery solutions, businesses can identify potential issues before they escalate, ensuring that the organization is well-prepared for any unexpected events.

In addition to testing the backup processes, it is crucial to document the recovery procedures clearly. This documentation should include step-by-step instructions for restoring Active Directory in various scenarios, such as a single object recovery or a full domain restore. By preparing detailed recovery plans, IT professionals can streamline the restoration process, reducing the time and effort required during an actual crisis. Furthermore, conducting regular training sessions based on these documented procedures ensures that all team members are familiar with the recovery protocols, thereby enhancing overall organizational readiness.

Maintaining recovery solutions goes beyond just testing and documentation. IT professionals must also keep abreast of changes in their Active Directory environment, such as updates to group policies or modifications to the AD schema. These changes can affect recovery strategies and may require adjustments to the existing backup and recovery plans. Implementing a change management process that includes regular reviews of the recovery solutions in conjunction with any changes made to the Active Directory infrastructure will help ensure ongoing alignment and effectiveness of the recovery strategy.

Finally, organizations should consider integrating their Active Directory recovery solutions with cloud-based services, especially as many small businesses migrate to hybrid environments. Cloud platforms often provide additional layers of redundancy and security, making them a valuable component of a comprehensive disaster recovery plan. Utilizing PowerShell scripts to automate the synchronization of local AD data with Azure AD can enhance recovery options and provide a more seamless restoration experience. By combining traditional recovery methods with modern cloud solutions, businesses can fortify their defenses against potential disruptions while optimizing their data management strategies.

ISSO-TECH

VICTOR P HENDERSON | ISSO-TECH ENTERPRISES™
CERTIFIED ETHICAL HACKER C|EH

ISSO-TECH PRESS™

CHAPTER 09
CLOUD SERVICES

CHAPTER 9 | CLOUD SERVICES
AZURE AD INTERGRATION

Integrating Active Directory with Azure AD

Integrating Active Directory (AD) with Azure Active Directory (Azure AD) allows you to extend your on-premises AD infrastructure to the cloud, providing seamless access to cloud-based applications and resources. Here's how you can integrate AD with Azure AD:

1. Azure AD Connect:

- Install and configure Azure AD Connect on a server in your on-premises AD environment.
- Azure AD Connect is a tool that synchronizes user accounts, groups, and attributes between your on-premises AD and Azure AD.

2. Configure Synchronization:

- During the Azure AD Connect setup, select the synchronization options that best fit your organization's requirements.
- You can choose to synchronize all user accounts and groups or filter based on specific criteria.

3. Single Sign-On (SSO):

- Configure Azure AD Connect to enable SSO for your users.
- This allows users to sign in to Azure AD-connected applications using their on-premises AD credentials.

4. Password Hash Synchronization:

- Enable password hash synchronization to synchronize user passwords between on-premises AD and Azure AD.

- This allows users to sign in to Azure AD-connected applications with the same password they use for on-premises resources.

5. Active Directory Federation Services (AD FS):
- If you require more advanced authentication scenarios, such as federated authentication or SSO with non-Microsoft applications, you can deploy AD FS.
- AD FS acts as a federation service that authenticates users against on-premises AD and issues security tokens for SSO.

6. User Account Provisioning:
- Azure AD Connect can be configured to automatically provision user accounts and groups from on-premises AD to Azure AD.
- This ensures that user accounts are kept up to date across both environments.

7. Conditional Access:
- Use Azure AD Conditional Access policies to enforce access controls based on user, device, location, and other factors.
- Conditional Access policies help ensure that only authorized users and devices can access your resources.

8. Monitoring and Reporting:
- Monitor the synchronization process and health of your Azure AD Connect installation using the Azure AD Connect Health tool.
- Use Azure AD reports to track user and group synchronization, sign-in activity, and other relevant metrics.

By integrating Active Directory with Azure AD, you can provide your users with a seamless and secure authentication experience across both on-premises and cloud-based resources.

@ISSO.TECH.ENTERPRISES

- Implementing hybrid identity solutions
Implementing a hybrid identity solution involves integrating your on-premises Active Directory (AD) environment with Azure Active Directory (Azure AD) to provide seamless authentication and access to resources both on-premises and in the cloud. Here's a general overview of the steps involved in implementing a hybrid identity solution:

1. Assessment and Planning:
- Conduct a thorough assessment of your current AD environment, including domain structure, user accounts, groups, and permissions.
- Identify the requirements and objectives of your hybrid identity solution, including which resources will be accessed both on-premises and in the cloud.

2. Azure AD Connect Installation:
- Install and configure Azure AD Connect on a server in your on-premises AD environment.
- Azure AD Connect is used to synchronize user accounts, groups, and attributes between on-premises AD and Azure AD.

3. Synchronization Configuration:
- Configure Azure AD Connect to synchronize user accounts, groups, and other relevant attributes between on-premises AD and Azure AD.
- Customize synchronization settings based on your organization's requirements, such as filtering user accounts or excluding specific attributes.

4. Single Sign-On (SSO):

- Configure Azure AD Connect to enable Single Sign-On (SSO) for your users.
- SSO allows users to sign in to Azure AD-connected applications using their on-premises AD credentials.

5. Password Hash Synchronization:

- Enable password hash synchronization to synchronize user passwords between on-premises AD and Azure AD.
- This allows users to sign in to Azure AD-connected applications with the same password they use for on-premises resources.

6. Active Directory Federation Services (AD FS) (Optional):

- If you require more advanced authentication scenarios, such as federated authentication or SSO with non-Microsoft applications, you can deploy AD FS.
- AD FS acts as a federation service that authenticates users against on-premises AD and issues security tokens for SSO.

7. Testing and Validation:

- Test the hybrid identity solution in a controlled environment to ensure that synchronization, SSO, and other features work as expected.
- Validate that users can access on-premises and cloud-based resources seamlessly using their AD credentials.

8. Deployment and Rollout:

- Once testing is successful, deploy the hybrid identity solution in your production environment.
- Plan a rollout strategy to gradually migrate users and resources to the hybrid identity solution while minimizing disruptions to users.

@ISSO.TECH.ENTERPRISES

9. Monitoring and Maintenance:

- Monitor the synchronization process, SSO functionality, and overall health of the hybrid identity solution.

- Perform regular maintenance tasks, such as updating Azure AD Connect and monitoring security alerts and advisories.

By following these steps, you can successfully implement a hybrid identity solution that integrates your on-premises AD environment with Azure AD, providing your organization with a secure and seamless authentication experience across both environments.

- Managing identities in a cloud environment
Managing identities in a cloud environment, such as Azure Active Directory (Azure AD), involves ensuring secure access to cloud-based resources for users and devices. Here are key aspects of managing identities in a cloud environment:

1. User Identity Lifecycle Management:

- Provision and deprovision user accounts based on organizational requirements.
- Ensure that user accounts are properly assigned to roles and groups to access relevant resources.

2. Access Control and Permissions:

- Define access control policies to manage who can access which resources.
- Use role-based access control (RBAC) to assign permissions based on user roles and responsibilities.

3. Single Sign-On (SSO):
- Enable SSO to allow users to sign in once and access multiple applications without needing to sign in again.
- Configure SSO for both cloud-based and on-premises applications.

4. Multi-Factor Authentication (MFA):
- Implement MFA to add an extra layer of security to user sign-ins.
- Require users to provide additional verification, such as a code sent to their mobile device, in addition to their password.

5. Identity Federation:
- Establish federation trust relationships with other identity providers (IdPs) to enable users to use their existing credentials to access cloud resources.
- Ensure secure authentication and communication between the IdPs and your cloud environment.

6. Identity Governance:
- Implement policies and procedures for managing and governing identities in your cloud environment.
- Define and enforce policies for user access, permissions, and compliance requirements.

7. Identity Lifecycle Automation:
- Automate identity lifecycle management tasks, such as user provisioning and deprovisioning, to improve efficiency and reduce errors.
- Use automation tools and scripts to streamline identity management processes.

@ISSO.TECH.ENTERPRISES

8. Identity Monitoring and Reporting:

- Monitor user activity and access patterns to detect and respond to suspicious or unauthorized behavior.
- Generate reports on identity-related metrics, such as user logins, access requests, and compliance status.

9. Security Best Practices:

- Implement security best practices for managing identities, such as regular password changes, least privilege access, and regular security assessments.
- Stay updated with security patches and updates to protect against vulnerabilities.

By effectively managing identities in a cloud environment, organizations can ensure secure and efficient access to resources while maintaining compliance with regulatory requirements and internal policies.

ACTIVE DIRECTORY WITH AZURE AD

Understanding Azure Active Directory

Azure Active Directory (Azure AD) is a cloud-based identity and access management service that plays a pivotal role in modern IT environments. For small businesses and IT professionals, Azure AD is not merely an extension of traditional Active Directory; it represents a robust solution that addresses the evolving needs of identity management in a cloud-centric world. By providing significant capabilities such as single sign-on, multifactor authentication, and conditional access policies, Azure AD allows organizations to securely manage user access to a plethora of applications while streamlining operational efficiency.

One of the fundamental differences between traditional Active Directory and Azure AD lies in their architecture. Traditional Active Directory is primarily designed for on-premises environments, relying on a domain controller to authenticate and authorize users within a local network. Conversely, Azure AD operates as a multi-tenant cloud service, enabling users to authenticate from anywhere, at any time, using various devices. This flexibility is particularly beneficial for small businesses that may not have the resources for extensive on-premises infrastructure. Understanding this distinction is crucial for IT professionals as they strategize their identity management approach in the cloud.

Security is paramount in any identity management system, and Azure AD incorporates various features to enhance security postures. For instance, it supports advanced security protocols,

such as OAuth 2.0 and OpenID Connect, which facilitate secure communication between applications and the identity provider. Furthermore, Azure AD includes built-in monitoring and logging capabilities that are essential for auditing and compliance, allowing organizations to track user activity and access patterns effectively. Small businesses can leverage these security features to fortify their defenses against unauthorized access and data breaches, which are increasingly common in today's digital landscape.

Integrating Azure AD with existing on-premises Active Directory environments can yield significant benefits, particularly for organizations looking to migrate to the cloud or enhance their hybrid infrastructure. This integration allows for seamless synchronization of user accounts, groups, and passwords, ensuring a consistent experience for users transitioning between on-premises and cloud resources. Additionally, understanding how to effectively manage Group Policy settings in conjunction with Azure AD can help IT professionals maintain compliance and enforce security policies across their IT environment.

Finally, the automation of Active Directory tasks using PowerShell in conjunction with Azure AD presents an opportunity for IT professionals to boost efficiency and streamline operations. PowerShell provides a powerful scripting environment that can be utilized to automate routine tasks such as user provisioning, group management, and auditing processes in both traditional and cloud-based environments. By mastering these automation techniques, network and system engineers can not only reduce the potential for human error but also free up valuable time to focus on strategic initiatives that drive business growth. Understanding Azure Active Directory and its capabilities is essential for any organization looking to thrive in a digital-first landscape.

Synchronization Strategies

In the realm of managing Active Directory (AD), synchronization strategies play a pivotal role in ensuring that data remains consistent across various environments and platforms. For small businesses and IT professionals, mastering synchronization techniques can significantly enhance operational efficiency and data integrity. This subchapter delves into the various synchronization strategies that can be employed to streamline Active Directory tasks, with a focus on automation using PowerShell. By effectively leveraging these strategies, network and system engineers can minimize errors and reduce the time spent on manual processes.

One of the foundational synchronization strategies involves using PowerShell cmdlets to automate the synchronization of user accounts, groups, and policies between on-premises Active Directory and cloud environments, particularly Azure AD. This approach not only simplifies the management of user identities but also ensures that security policies remain consistent across different platforms. For small businesses transitioning to cloud services, understanding how to implement these automated synchronization processes is essential. PowerShell scripts can be crafted to regularly check for discrepancies and apply necessary updates, thus maintaining a cohesive identity management framework.

@ISSO.TECH.ENTERPRISES

Another critical aspect of synchronization strategies is the implementation of Group Policy Objects (GPOs) across multiple sites and domains. By utilizing PowerShell for automating the deployment and updating of GPOs, IT professionals can ensure that security settings and configurations are uniformly applied. This is particularly important for compliance and auditing purposes, as inconsistent policies can lead to vulnerabilities. Establishing a robust synchronization schedule for GPOs not only fosters a secure environment but also eases the administrative burden on network engineers, allowing them to focus on more strategic initiatives.

Troubleshooting synchronization issues is a necessary skill that every IT professional should master. Common problems such as replication failures and latency can hinder the seamless operation of Active Directory environments. By employing PowerShell, engineers can automate diagnostic tasks to quickly identify and resolve synchronization discrepancies. Regularly scheduled health checks and automated alerts can provide proactive monitoring, thereby minimizing downtime and ensuring that all changes in Active Directory are effectively propagated across all relevant systems.

Finally, adopting a comprehensive synchronization strategy that incorporates disaster recovery planning is crucial for small businesses. By establishing a reliable backup and restoration process for Active Directory, organizations can safeguard against data loss due to synchronization errors or failures. PowerShell scripts can facilitate the automation of backup routines and the validation of backup integrity, ensuring that businesses are prepared for any unforeseen circumstances. In conclusion, mastering synchronization strategies within Active Directory using PowerShell not only boosts efficiency but also enhances security and compliance for small businesses and IT professionals alike.

Managing Identities in a Hybrid Environment

Managing identities in a hybrid environment presents unique challenges and opportunities for small businesses and IT professionals. As organizations increasingly adopt cloud solutions alongside traditional on-premises infrastructures, the integration of Active Directory (AD) with cloud services like Azure AD becomes essential. This subchapter delves into effective strategies for managing identities across these diverse environments, ensuring security, compliance, and operational efficiency.

One of the primary considerations in a hybrid environment is the synchronization of identities between on-premises AD and Azure AD. Utilizing tools such as Azure AD Connect allows businesses to create a seamless experience for users while maintaining centralized management. This synchronization process ensures that user identities remain consistent across both environments, reducing the risk of discrepancies that can lead to security vulnerabilities. Regular monitoring and maintenance of synchronization processes are crucial to avoid potential issues that may arise from identity drift.

Security best practices must be at the forefront of identity management in a hybrid setup. Small businesses often face challenges related to limited resources, making it vital to implement robust security measures without overwhelming their IT teams. Multi-factor authentication (MFA) should be enforced to add an extra layer of protection, particularly for remote access scenarios. Additionally, regular audits of user permissions and roles can help identify potential security risks, ensuring that users have access only to the resources necessary for their roles.

Group Policy Management also plays a significant role in managing identities within a hybrid environment. By leveraging Group Policy Objects (GPOs), IT professionals can enforce security settings, software installation policies, and user configurations across both on-premises and cloud-based systems. This consistency helps maintain compliance with industry standards and internal policies, simplifying the management of user identities. Automation through PowerShell can enhance this process, allowing for the quick deployment of GPOs across multiple environments, thereby reducing manual workloads.

Troubleshooting identity-related issues is another critical aspect of managing a hybrid environment. IT professionals must be equipped to diagnose and resolve problems that may arise from the integration of on-premises and cloud services. Utilizing PowerShell scripts can aid in identifying discrepancies in user accounts, authentication failures, or synchronization problems. Developing a robust incident response plan that includes specific protocols for addressing identity management issues will ensure minimal downtime and maintain trust in the organization's IT infrastructure.

In conclusion, effective management of identities in a hybrid environment requires a strategic approach that combines synchronization, security best practices, Group Policy Management, and troubleshooting capabilities. For small businesses and IT professionals, embracing automation through PowerShell not only enhances efficiency but also mitigates the risks associated with identity management. By prioritizing these elements, organizations can foster a secure, compliant, and user-friendly environment that supports their operational goals.

ISSO-TECH

VICTOR P HENDERSON | ISSO-TECH ENTERPRISES™
CERTIFIED ETHICAL HACKER C|EH

ISSO-TECH PRESS™

CHAPTER 10
ACTIVE DIRECTORY
BEST PRACTICES

CHAPTER 10 | ACTIVE DIRECTORY BEST PRACTICES
FUTURE TRENDS

Best practices for managing Active Directory

Managing Active Directory (AD) effectively involves implementing a set of best practices to ensure security, performance, and reliability. Here are some key best practices for managing AD:

1. Regular Backups:

- Perform regular backups of AD database (NTDS.dit) and system state to protect against data loss.
- Test backups periodically to ensure they can be restored successfully.

2. Security Configuration:

- Implement strong password policies, such as password complexity and expiration settings.
- Enable auditing to track changes and access to AD objects.
- Disable unnecessary services and protocols to reduce the attack surface.

3. Group Policy Management:

- Use Group Policy Objects (GPOs) to manage and enforce security settings, software installation, and other configurations across your AD environment.
- Regularly review and update GPOs to reflect changes in security requirements.

VICTOR P HENDERSON | ISSO-TECH ENTERPRISES™
CERTIFIED ETHICAL HACKER C|EH

ISSO-TECH PRESS™

4. Patch Management:

- Keep AD servers up to date with the latest security patches and updates.
- Use a systematic approach for testing and deploying updates to minimize disruptions.

5. Monitor AD Health:

- Monitor the health of AD domain controllers, including replication status, performance metrics, and event logs.
- Use monitoring tools to detect and troubleshoot issues proactively.

6. Active Directory Sites and Services:

- Configure AD Sites and Services to optimize replication traffic and ensure efficient communication between domain controllers.
- Use site links and replication schedules to control how and when replication occurs.

7. Delegate Administrative Tasks:

- Use role-based access control (RBAC) to delegate administrative tasks to specific users or groups.
- Limit administrative privileges to minimize the risk of accidental or malicious changes.

8. Regular Audits and Reviews:

- Conduct regular security audits and reviews of AD configurations, permissions, and group memberships.
- Remove or disable unused accounts and permissions.

9. Disaster Recovery Planning:

- Develop and maintain a disaster recovery plan for AD, including procedures for restoring AD in the event of a failure.

- Test the disaster recovery plan regularly to ensure its effectiveness.

10. Training and Documentation:
- Provide training to IT staff on AD best practices, security policies, and procedures.
- Maintain up-to-date documentation of AD configurations, procedures, and policies.

By following these best practices, you can help ensure that your AD environment remains secure, reliable, and well-managed.
- Future trends in Active Directory

Active Directory (AD) continues to evolve to meet the changing needs of organizations. Some future trends and developments in AD include:

1. Cloud Integration:
- Increased integration between on-premises AD and cloud-based services, such as Azure Active Directory (Azure AD), to provide seamless access to resources in hybrid environments.

2. Identity Management as a Service (IDaaS):
- Growing adoption of IDaaS solutions, which provide cloud-based identity management services, including authentication, authorization, and access management.

3. Enhanced Security Features:
- Continued focus on enhancing security features, such as multi-factor authentication (MFA), conditional access, and privileged identity management (PIM), to protect against evolving cyber threats.

ISSO-TECH PRESS™

4. Simplified Management:

- Improved tools and interfaces for managing AD, making it easier for administrators to configure and maintain their AD environments.

5. Machine Learning and AI:

- Integration of machine learning and artificial intelligence (AI) technologies to improve identity and access management, including detecting and mitigating security threats.

6. Zero Trust Security Model:

- Adoption of the zero trust security model, which assumes that every user and device accessing the network is untrusted, leading to more granular access controls and continuous authentication.

7. Blockchain for Identity Management:

- Exploration of blockchain technology for decentralized and secure identity management, potentially reducing the reliance on centralized identity providers.

8. Compliance and Governance:

- Increased focus on compliance and governance requirements, with AD evolving to provide more robust auditing, reporting, and access control capabilities.

9. Containerization and Microservices:

- Adoption of containerization and microservices architectures for AD, enabling more flexible and scalable deployments in modern IT environments.

10. Integration with Other Services:
- Deeper integration with other Microsoft services, such as Office 365, Microsoft 365, and Azure services, to provide a more seamless and integrated user experience.

These trends indicate a continued evolution of Active Directory to meet the demands of modern IT environments, providing enhanced security, flexibility, and scalability for organizations.
- Conclusion and final thoughts

This book aims to provide a comprehensive guide to Microsoft Active Directory, covering everything from planning and deployment to advanced topics and best practices. It is designed for IT professionals, system administrators, and anyone looking to master Active Directory for their organization's infrastructure.

ISSO-TECH

229.320.151.6

CHAPTER 11
DIAGNOSTIC TECHNIQUES

@ISSO.TECH.ENTERPRISES

CHAPTER 11 | DIAGNOSTIC TECHNIQUES
TROUBLESHOOTING AND OPTIMIZATION

Introduction to active directory diagnostics
Importance of diagnostics in Active Directory
Diagnostics in Active Directory (AD) are crucial for maintaining a healthy and reliable directory service. They play a critical role in identifying and resolving issues that can impact the security, performance, and availability of AD. Here are some key reasons why diagnostics are important in AD:

1. Issue Identification: Diagnostics help identify problems within the AD environment, such as replication issues, DNS configuration errors, or database corruption.

2. Performance Monitoring: Diagnostics provide insights into the performance of AD services and help identify bottlenecks or issues that may be affecting performance.

3. Troubleshooting: When issues occur, diagnostics help troubleshoot the problem by providing detailed information about the root cause and potential solutions.

4. Proactive Maintenance: Regular diagnostics help detect and resolve issues before they escalate, ensuring that AD remains available and responsive.

5. Security: Diagnostics can help identify security vulnerabilities or unauthorized access attempts, allowing organizations to take appropriate action to secure AD.

6. Compliance: Diagnostics help ensure that AD complies with regulatory requirements and internal policies by monitoring access, changes, and other activities.

7. Data Integrity: Diagnostics help ensure the integrity of AD data by identifying and resolving issues such as replication conflicts or data corruption.

8. Capacity Planning: Diagnostics provide insights into the usage and capacity of AD services, helping organizations plan for future growth and resource requirements.

Overall, diagnostics are essential for maintaining a healthy and reliable Active Directory environment. They help organizations identify and resolve issues, ensure optimal performance and security, and comply with regulatory requirements.
- Common Active Directory issues

Active Directory (AD) is a robust and reliable directory service, but it can experience various issues that can impact its performance, security, and availability. Some common AD issues include:

1. Replication Issues:
- Replication failures can occur due to network connectivity issues, DNS problems, or conflicts between domain controllers (DCs).
- Symptoms include inconsistent data between DCs, errors in event logs related to replication, and issues with group policy application.

2. Authentication Problems:
- Users may experience authentication failures due to issues with their credentials, AD configuration, or network connectivity.

- Symptoms include users unable to log in, frequent password prompts, or slow authentication times.

3. DNS Configuration Errors:
- Incorrect DNS settings can cause AD issues, as AD heavily relies on DNS for name resolution.
- Symptoms include AD replication failures, authentication problems, and DNS-related errors in event logs.

4. DC Hardware Failures:
- Hardware failures on domain controllers can cause AD services to become unavailable.
- Symptoms include DCs not responding, errors related to hardware failures in event logs, and inability to access AD resources.

5. Permissions and Access Control Issues:
- Incorrectly configured permissions can lead to access issues for users and applications.
- Symptoms include users unable to access resources, errors related to permissions in event logs, and security breaches.

6. Group Policy Problems:
- Issues with group policies can cause incorrect settings to be applied or prevent policies from being applied.
- Symptoms include group policy application failures, inconsistent policy settings, and errors related to group policy processing in event logs.

7. Schema and Object Replication Issues:
- Problems with the AD schema or object replication can cause data inconsistencies or failures.

- Symptoms include errors related to schema replication or object replication in event logs, and inconsistencies in object attributes.

8. AD Database Corruption:

- The AD database (NTDS.dit) can become corrupted due to various reasons, such as hardware failures or software bugs.
- Symptoms include errors related to database corruption in event logs, replication failures, and issues with accessing AD objects.

9. Security Vulnerabilities:

- AD can be vulnerable to security threats, such as unauthorized access, malware, or insider threats.
- Symptoms include suspicious activity in event logs, unauthorized changes to AD objects, and compromised credentials.

10. Performance Degradation:

- AD performance can degrade over time due to factors such as increased load, inefficient configurations, or hardware limitations.
- Symptoms include slow authentication times, delays in accessing AD resources, and high CPU or memory usage on DCs.

These are just some of the common issues that can affect Active Directory. Proper monitoring, maintenance, and troubleshooting are essential to keep AD running smoothly and prevent or resolve these issues.
- Overview of diagnostic tools and techniques

Diagnosing issues in Active Directory (AD) requires a combination of tools and techniques to identify and resolve problems. Here's an overview of common diagnostic tools and techniques used for AD troubleshooting:

@ISSO.TECH.ENTERPRISES

1. Event Viewer:

- Event Viewer is a built-in Windows tool that logs events and errors from various sources, including AD.
- Use Event Viewer to look for errors or warnings related to AD services, replication, authentication, and other AD-related activities.

2. DCDiag:

- DCDiag is a command-line tool used to diagnose domain controller issues.
- Use DCDiag to check the health of domain controllers, replication status, DNS configuration, and other AD-related tests.

3. Repadmin:

- Repadmin is a command-line tool used to manage and diagnose replication issues in AD.
- Use Repadmin to check replication status, force replication between domain controllers, and view replication metadata.

4. ADSIEdit:

- ADSIEdit is a Windows support tool used to manage AD objects and attributes.
- Use ADSIEdit to view and modify AD objects, check replication metadata, and troubleshoot AD configuration issues.

5. AD Replication Status Tool:

- The AD Replication Status Tool is a graphical tool that provides an overview of the replication status of domain controllers in an AD forest.
- Use the tool to quickly identify replication failures and latency issues.

6. Network Monitor/Wireshark:

- Network monitoring tools like Network Monitor or Wireshark can be used to capture and analyze network traffic related to AD communications.
- Use these tools to troubleshoot network connectivity issues, DNS problems, and other network-related AD issues.

7. Performance Monitor:

- Performance Monitor is a Windows tool used to monitor and analyze system performance metrics.
- Use Performance Monitor to monitor AD-related performance counters, such as LDAP queries, replication latency, and CPU/memory usage on domain controllers.

8. Active Directory Administrative Center:

- Active Directory Administrative Center (ADAC) is a graphical management tool for AD.
- Use ADAC to perform common AD management tasks, view object properties, and troubleshoot AD configuration issues.

9. PowerShell:

- PowerShell can be used to perform various AD management and diagnostic tasks using cmdlets.
- Use PowerShell to query AD information, check replication status, and perform other AD-related tasks.

10. Third-Party Tools:

- There are many third-party tools available for AD diagnostics and monitoring, such as Quest Active Administrator, ManageEngine ADManager Plus, and Netwrix Auditor.
- These tools provide additional features and capabilities for AD troubleshooting and management.

When diagnosing issues in Active Directory, it's important to use a combination of these tools and techniques to identify and resolve problems effectively.

TROUBLESHOOTING ACTIVE DIRECTORY ISSUES

Common Active Directory Problems

Active Directory (AD) serves as the backbone for identity and access management in many organizations, yet it is not without its challenges. Small businesses, IT professionals, network engineers, and system engineers frequently encounter a range of common problems that can impede the functionality and security of their AD environments. Understanding these issues is essential for implementing effective solutions and ensuring that Active Directory operates smoothly. This subchapter delves into some prevalent problems that may arise in Active Directory and offers insights on how to address them.

One of the most common issues faced by organizations is user account management. As teams grow and evolve, maintaining accurate and up-to-date user accounts can become increasingly complex. Problems such as orphaned accounts, where former employees' accounts remain active, can pose significant security risks. Additionally, managing group memberships effectively is critical to ensuring that users have appropriate access rights. Failing to remove users from groups after they leave the organization or change roles can lead to unauthorized access to sensitive resources. Automating user account provisioning and deprovisioning through PowerShell scripts can significantly alleviate these issues, enhancing both efficiency and security.

Another frequent problem is Group Policy Management, which is vital for enforcing security settings and configurations across an organization. Misconfigurations within Group Policies can lead to

@ISSO.TECH.ENTERPRISES

inconsistent application of settings, resulting in potential vulnerabilities. For example, if a policy intended to enforce password complexity is not applied correctly, it may leave user accounts susceptible to attacks. Regular auditing of Group Policies and utilizing PowerShell cmdlets to automate compliance checks can help identify and rectify these issues before they escalate. Understanding how to leverage PowerShell for Group Policy management can streamline these processes, ensuring that security policies are consistently applied.

Active Directory replication issues also present significant challenges, particularly in environments with multiple domain controllers. Replication failures can lead to discrepancies in user authentication and access rights, causing confusion and downtime. Troubleshooting these replication problems requires a thorough understanding of the underlying topology and the ability to diagnose connectivity issues. PowerShell offers powerful tools for monitoring replication health and diagnosing problems, allowing IT professionals to proactively manage their AD environments. By implementing automated monitoring scripts, businesses can quickly identify and resolve replication issues, thereby maintaining a stable and secure Active Directory infrastructure.

Lastly, disaster recovery planning is an often-overlooked aspect of Active Directory management. Many small businesses lack a comprehensive strategy for recovering AD in the event of a failure or breach. Without proper backups and recovery procedures, organizations risk losing critical access to resources and data. Implementing regular backup schedules and testing recovery processes are essential steps in ensuring business continuity. PowerShell can play a vital role in automating backup tasks and performing health checks on the Active Directory environment, making it easier for businesses to prepare for potential disasters and ensure swift recovery.

In conclusion, while Active Directory is a powerful tool for managing user identities and access, it is not immune to challenges. Common problems such as user account management, Group Policy misconfigurations, replication issues, and inadequate disaster recovery planning can hinder the effectiveness of AD. By understanding these issues and utilizing PowerShell for automation, small businesses and IT professionals can enhance the security and efficiency of their Active Directory environments. As organizations continue to evolve, investing time in mastering these aspects of Active Directory will ultimately lead to a more robust and secure IT infrastructure.

Tools and Techniques for Troubleshooting

In the realm of Active Directory (AD) management, troubleshooting is an essential skill for IT professionals, particularly within small businesses where resources may be limited and efficiency is paramount. Effective troubleshooting techniques can significantly reduce downtime and enhance the stability of the network. This subchapter will explore the fundamental tools and techniques that can aid in diagnosing and resolving common Active Directory issues, empowering IT staff to maintain a robust and secure environment.

@ISSO.TECH.ENTERPRISES

One of the primary tools for troubleshooting Active Directory is PowerShell. This versatile scripting language allows IT professionals to execute complex commands and automate tasks that would otherwise require extensive manual effort. For instance, commands like `Get-ADUser` or `Get-ADGroup` can quickly reveal the status of user accounts and group memberships, helping to identify potential misconfigurations. Additionally, PowerShell's ability to access Event Logs using `Get-WinEvent` can provide critical insights into authentication failures, replication issues, and other anomalies affecting AD performance.

Another essential component in the troubleshooting toolkit is the Active Directory Users and Computers (ADUC) console. This graphical interface provides a clear view of the AD structure and is invaluable for managing users, groups, and organizational units (OUs). The ADUC console allows for real-time modifications and can help troubleshoot issues related to user permissions, group policies, and overall directory health. Utilizing the "Users" and "Computers" containers effectively can streamline the identification of account issues and enhance the management of security groups.

In addition to these tools, understanding the underlying protocols that facilitate Active Directory operations is crucial for effective troubleshooting. Familiarity with Kerberos and NTLM, the primary authentication protocols used by Active Directory, enables IT professionals to diagnose authentication-related problems more efficiently. For example, issues such as failed logins can often be traced back to expired passwords, account lockouts, or misconfigured service principals. Knowledge of these protocols equips network engineers with the insights needed to resolve complex authentication scenarios.

Finally, integrating third-party monitoring and diagnostic tools can enhance an organization's troubleshooting capabilities. Tools such as SolarWinds and Quest Active Roles provide comprehensive monitoring solutions that can proactively identify issues before they escalate. These platforms often include features like performance analytics, alerts for unusual behavior, and detailed reporting, which are invaluable for maintaining compliance and security. By combining native Active Directory tools with advanced monitoring solutions, IT professionals can create a robust troubleshooting framework that not only resolves issues but also anticipates potential problems, ensuring a more resilient Active Directory environment.

Best Practices for Resolving Issues

Resolving issues in Active Directory (AD) environments is a critical skill for IT professionals, particularly within small businesses where resources may be limited. Effective problem resolution not only minimizes downtime but also ensures that the integrity and security of the AD environment are maintained. Employing best practices in troubleshooting helps streamline the process and enhances overall efficiency. This subchapter outlines essential strategies for resolving AD-related issues, focusing on systematic approaches, the use of PowerShell for automation, and maintaining comprehensive documentation.

@ISSO.TECH.ENTERPRISES

A systematic approach to troubleshooting begins with a clear understanding of the problem. IT professionals should gather as much information as possible before diving into potential solutions. This includes identifying the symptoms, understanding the impact on users, and checking for any recent changes in the environment. Utilizing tools such as the Event Viewer and PowerShell cmdlets can provide valuable insights into underlying issues. By establishing a baseline of expected behavior and comparing it with current performance, network engineers can pinpoint deviations that may indicate the source of the problem.

PowerShell is an invaluable tool for automating Active Directory tasks and can significantly enhance the troubleshooting process. By creating scripts that automate common diagnostic tasks, IT professionals can save time and reduce the potential for human error. For instance, automating the collection of user account information, group memberships, and permissions can provide a quick overview of an affected account's status. Additionally, PowerShell can be leveraged to reset accounts, update attributes, or restore deleted objects, all of which can expedite issue resolution. Familiarity with PowerShell scripting not only boosts efficiency but also empowers IT professionals to address issues proactively before they escalate.

Documentation is often overlooked but remains a cornerstone of effective issue resolution. Maintaining detailed records of problems encountered, steps taken, and resolutions applied can serve as a valuable reference for future incidents. This practice not only aids in the immediate troubleshooting process but also contributes to a knowledge base that can be utilized across the organization. Establishing standardized documentation templates for common issues ensures consistency and allows for easier onboarding of new IT staff. Furthermore, regular reviews of documented issues can reveal patterns that inform preventive measures, ultimately reducing the frequency of similar problems.

Collaboration and communication within the IT team and across departments are essential for resolving issues effectively. Small businesses often require team members to wear multiple hats, making it crucial to foster an environment where knowledge sharing is encouraged. Utilizing collaboration tools and platforms can facilitate real-time communication and allow for the rapid exchange of information during troubleshooting efforts. Engaging with peers or seeking advice from online communities can also enhance problem-solving capabilities, as diverse perspectives may lead to innovative solutions. Establishing clear lines of communication ensures that all stakeholders are informed about ongoing issues and resolutions, promoting a unified approach to problem-solving.

In conclusion, resolving Active Directory issues requires a combination of systematic troubleshooting, effective use of automation tools like PowerShell, thorough documentation, and collaborative efforts. By adhering to these best practices, IT professionals can enhance their efficiency and effectiveness in managing AD environments. Small businesses stand to benefit significantly from these strategies, ultimately improving their operational resilience and ensuring a secure and stable IT infrastructure. Emphasizing these practices not only leads to quicker resolutions but also fosters a culture of continuous improvement within the organization.

ISSO-TECH

VICTOR P HENDERSON | ISSO-TECH ENTERPRISES™
CERTIFIED ETHICAL HACKER C|EH

ISSO-TECH PRESS™

229.320.151.6

CHAPTER 12
PERFORMANCE

CHAPTER 12 | PERFORMANCE
MONITORING AND ANALYSIS

Performance monitoring tools
Performance monitoring tools help you understand and optimize the performance of your Active Directory (AD) environment. Here are some commonly used performance monitoring tools for AD:

1. Performance Monitor (Perfmon):
- Built-in Windows tool for monitoring various performance counters related to AD, such as CPU usage, memory usage, disk activity, and network traffic.
- Use Perfmon to identify performance bottlenecks and troubleshoot performance issues in real time.

2. Active Directory Performance Testing Tool (ADTest):
- A tool provided by Microsoft to simulate load on an AD infrastructure and measure its performance.
- Use ADTest to evaluate the performance of AD under different conditions and identify potential scalability issues.

3. Active Directory Replication Status Tool (ADREPLSTATUS):
- A graphical tool provided by Microsoft to monitor the replication status of domain controllers in an AD forest.
- Use ADREPLSTATUS to identify replication failures and latency issues, which can impact AD performance.

4. Windows Performance Toolkit (WPT):
- A set of tools provided by Microsoft for analyzing and diagnosing Windows performance issues, including AD.

- Use WPT to capture and analyze performance data, identify performance bottlenecks, and troubleshoot performance problems.

5. Quest Spotlight on Active Directory:
- A third-party monitoring tool that provides real-time visibility into the performance and health of AD.
- Use Spotlight to monitor AD performance metrics, diagnose issues, and optimize AD performance.

6. ManageEngine ADManager Plus:
- A comprehensive AD management and reporting tool that includes performance monitoring capabilities.
- Use ADManager Plus to monitor AD performance metrics, generate performance reports, and troubleshoot performance issues.

7. Netwrix Auditor for Active Directory:
- A security and compliance monitoring tool that includes performance monitoring features for AD.
- Use Netwrix Auditor to monitor AD performance metrics, track changes to AD objects, and detect security threats.

8. SolarWinds Server & Application Monitor (SAM):
- A comprehensive monitoring tool that includes performance monitoring capabilities for AD.
- Use SAM to monitor AD performance metrics, track resource usage, and troubleshoot performance issues.

These tools can help you monitor and optimize the performance of your Active Directory environment, ensuring that it remains efficient and reliable.
- Identifying and troubleshooting performance bottlenecks

@ISSO.TECH.ENTERPRISES

Identifying and troubleshooting performance bottlenecks in Active Directory (AD) is essential for maintaining optimal performance and user experience. Here are the key steps to identify and address performance issues:

1. Monitor Performance Metrics:
- Use performance monitoring tools like Performance Monitor (Perfmon) to monitor key performance counters related to AD, such as CPU usage, memory usage, disk activity, and network traffic.
- Look for patterns or spikes in performance metrics that indicate potential bottlenecks.

2. Identify the Scope:
- Determine if the performance issue is affecting a specific domain controller, a specific AD operation, or the entire AD forest.
- This will help narrow down the scope of the issue and focus your troubleshooting efforts.

3. Check Replication Status:
- Use tools like Active Directory Replication Status Tool (ADREPLSTATUS) to check the replication status of domain controllers.
- Replication issues can cause performance bottlenecks, so ensure that replication is healthy.

4. Review Event Logs:
- Check the Windows event logs on domain controllers for any errors or warnings related to AD services, replication, or performance.
- Look for recurring events that may indicate underlying issues.

5. Review AD Infrastructure:

- Review the AD infrastructure, including the number of domain controllers, their placement in sites, and the configuration of AD sites and subnets.
- Ensure that the infrastructure is designed to support the workload and is properly configured for efficient replication and authentication.

6. Check DNS Configuration:

- AD heavily relies on DNS for name resolution, so ensure that DNS is properly configured and functioning correctly.
- Check for DNS issues that could impact AD performance, such as incorrect DNS settings or DNS server availability.

7. Monitor Active Directory Database (NTDS.dit):

- Monitor the size and growth rate of the AD database (NTDS.dit) to ensure it is not reaching its capacity limits.
- Consider defragmenting the database if it becomes fragmented to improve performance.

8. Optimize Group Policy Objects (GPOs):

- Review and optimize Group Policy Objects (GPOs) to reduce the number of policies applied and their complexity.
- Excessive GPOs or complex policies can impact AD performance.

9. Check Hardware Resources:

- Ensure that domain controllers have adequate hardware resources, such as CPU, memory, and disk space, to handle the workload.
- Consider upgrading hardware if it is insufficient for the workload.

@ISSO.TECH.ENTERPRISES

10. Review Application and Service Dependencies:
- Identify and review applications or services that rely on AD for authentication or other services.
- Ensure that these applications or services are not causing excessive load or performance issues in AD.

11. Implement Performance Tuning:
- Implement performance tuning recommendations based on your findings, such as optimizing AD replication, adjusting DNS settings, or tuning hardware resources.
- Monitor the impact of these changes to ensure they improve performance.

By following these steps, you can identify and troubleshoot performance bottlenecks in Active Directory, helping to improve the overall performance and reliability of your AD environment.
- Optimizing Active Directory performance
Optimizing Active Directory (AD) performance involves several key strategies to ensure that AD services operate efficiently and effectively. Here are some best practices for optimizing AD performance:

1. Hardware Resources:
- Ensure that domain controllers have adequate CPU, memory, and disk resources to handle the workload.
- Consider using faster disks (e.g., SSDs) for the AD database (NTDS.dit) and logs to improve read/write performance.

2. Active Directory Database (NTDS.dit):
- Monitor the size and growth rate of the AD database and consider defragmenting the database if it becomes fragmented.

- Regularly perform maintenance tasks, such as integrity checks and backups, to ensure database health.

3. Indexing:
- Index frequently searched attributes to improve query performance.
- Use tools like the Active Directory Schema Analyzer (ADSA) to identify attributes that can benefit from indexing.

4. Replication:
- Ensure that replication between domain controllers is efficient and reliable.
- Monitor replication status and address any issues that may impact performance.

5. DNS Configuration:
- Ensure that DNS is properly configured and functioning correctly, as AD heavily relies on DNS for name resolution.
- Use forwarders or conditional forwarding to improve DNS query performance.

6. Group Policy Objects (GPOs):
- Review and optimize Group Policy Objects (GPOs) to reduce the number of policies applied and their complexity.
- Consolidate GPOs where possible to reduce the processing overhead on client machines.

7. Active Directory Sites and Services:
- Ensure that AD sites and subnets are properly configured to optimize replication and authentication traffic.

@ISSO.TECH.ENTERPRISES

- Use site links and replication schedules to control how and when replication occurs.

8. Monitoring and Maintenance:
- Regularly monitor AD performance metrics, such as CPU and memory usage, replication status, and database size.
- Perform regular maintenance tasks, such as database defragmentation and integrity checks, to ensure optimal performance.

9. Security Best Practices:
- Implement security best practices to protect AD from unauthorized access and malicious attacks.
- Regularly review and update security policies and access controls.

10. Consider Virtualization:
- Consider virtualizing domain controllers to improve scalability and flexibility.
- Ensure that virtualized domain controllers have adequate resources and are properly configured for optimal performance.

By implementing these best practices, you can optimize the performance of your Active Directory environment, ensuring that it operates efficiently and reliably to meet the needs of your organization.

ISSO-TECH

VICTOR P HENDERSON | ISSO-TECH ENTERPRISES™
CERTIFIED ETHICAL HACKER C|EH

ISSO-TECH PRESS™

229.320.151.8

CHAPTER 13
REPLICATION

CHAPTER 13 | REPLICATION
TROUBLESHOOTING AND VERIFICATION

Understanding Active Directory replication

Active Directory (AD) replication is the process of synchronizing changes made to AD objects (such as users, groups, and computer accounts) between domain controllers (DCs) within a domain or across domains in a forest. Replication ensures that all DCs in a domain or forest have up-to-date and consistent information.

Key aspects of AD replication include:

1. Replication Topology:
- AD replication follows a specific topology that determines how changes are replicated between DCs.
- The replication topology is based on site links, which define the physical network connections between AD sites.

2. Replication Protocols:
- AD uses the Remote Procedure Call (RPC) and the Simple Mail Transfer Protocol (SMTP) for replication.
- RPC is used for intrasite replication, while SMTP is used for intersite replication.

3. Replication Types:
- There are two types of replications in AD:
- Intrasite replication: Occurs within the same site and is triggered by the change notification process.
- Intersite replication: Occurs between different sites and is triggered by the schedule defined in site link settings.

4. Replication Process:

- When a change is made to an AD object on a DC, the DC marks the object as "dirty" and replicates the change to other DCs in the same site (intrasite replication) or across sites (intersite replication).
- The replication process involves several steps, including update notification, data request, data transfer, and acknowledgement.

5. Replication Partners:

- Each DC has replication partners that it replicates with.
- Replication partners are determined by the replication topology and are typically other DCs within the same site or across sites.

6. Bridgehead Servers:

- Bridgehead servers are DCs that act as intermediaries for replication traffic between sites.
- Bridgehead servers are responsible for receiving and forwarding replication traffic between sites.

7. Monitoring and Troubleshooting:

- Monitoring replication status is important to ensure that changes are replicated successfully and in a timely manner.
- Troubleshooting replication issues involves checking replication status, event logs, and using tools like Repadmin and Active Directory Replication Status Tool (ADREPLSTATUS).

Understanding AD replication is crucial for maintaining a healthy and reliable AD environment. Proper configuration and monitoring of replication ensure that changes are propagated efficiently and consistently across all DCs.
- Diagnosing and resolving replication issues

Diagnosing and resolving replication issues in Active Directory (AD) is critical to maintaining a healthy and reliable AD environment. Here's a step-by-step guide to diagnosing and resolving common replication issues:

1. Check Replication Status:
- Use the Repadmin tool to check the replication status between domain controllers (DCs). Run the following command:
repadmin /replsummary
- Look for any errors or warnings that indicate replication issues, such as "Last replication error" or "Last replication latency."

2. Review Event Logs:
- Check the Directory Service event logs on DCs for any replication-related errors or warnings.
- Look for event IDs such as 1311, 1566, or 1864, which indicate replication problems.

3. Check Replication Topology:
- Use the Active Directory Sites and Services console to review the replication topology.
- Ensure that site links are configured correctly and that there are no connectivity issues between sites.

4. Check DNS Configuration:
- Ensure that DNS is properly configured and that DCs can resolve each other's names.
- Check for DNS-related errors in the event logs and resolve any issues.

5. Verify Network Connectivity:
- Ensure that there are no network connectivity issues between DCs.
- Use tools like Ping or Tracert to verify connectivity and resolve any issues.

6. Check Replication Schedule:
- Verify the replication schedule for site links in Active Directory Sites and Services.
- Ensure that replication schedules are configured appropriately for your environment.

7. Force Replication:
- If replication is not occurring as expected, you can force replication using the Repadmin tool. Run the following command on the destination DC:
repadmin /syncall /AdeP
- This command forces replication of all partitions from all DCs.

8. Monitor Replication Health:
- Use tools like Active Directory Replication Status Tool (ADREPLSTATUS) to monitor the health of replication.
- Look for trends or patterns that may indicate ongoing replication issues.

9. Review Firewall and Security Settings:
- Ensure that firewall settings allow replication traffic between DCs.
- Review security settings, such as permissions and group membership, that may impact replication.

@ISSO.TECH.ENTERPRISES

10. Perform Metadata Cleanup:

- If a DC has been removed from the network without being properly demoted, perform metadata cleanup to remove lingering objects.
- Use the Ntdsutil tool to perform metadata cleanup.

11. Resolve Any Lingering Objects:

- If there are lingering objects in AD, use the Repadmin tool to remove them.
- Run the following command on a DC that has the lingering object:

```
repadmin /removelingeringobjects <DC Naming Context> <Source DC> <GUID>
```

12. Verify Replication Health:

- After resolving replication issues, monitor the replication health to ensure that the issues have been resolved.
- Continue to monitor replication health regularly to catch any new issues early.

By following these steps, you can diagnose and resolve replication issues in Active Directory, ensuring that your AD environment remains healthy and reliable.

- Monitoring replication health

Monitoring replication health in Active Directory (AD) is essential to ensure that changes are replicated correctly and in a timely manner across all domain controllers (DCs). Here's how you can monitor replication health:

1. Repadmin Tool:
- Use the Repadmin tool to check the status of replication between DCs. Run the following command:
```
repadmin /replsummary
```

- This command provides a summary of the replication status, including any errors or warnings.

2. Active Directory Sites and Services:
- Use the Active Directory Sites and Services console to view the replication topology and replication connections between DCs.
- Look for any errors or warnings in the connections.

3. Event Viewer:
- Check the Directory Service event logs on DCs for any replication-related errors or warnings.
- Look for event IDs such as 1311, 1566, or 1864, which indicate replication problems.

4. Replication Status Tool (ADREPLSTATUS):
- Use the Active Directory Replication Status Tool (ADREPLSTATUS) to monitor the replication status of DCs.
- The tool provides a graphical view of the replication status and can help identify replication issues.

5. Performance Monitor (Perfmon):
- Monitor performance counters related to replication, such as Replication Queue Length and Replication Latency, using Perfmon.
- Look for trends or spikes in these counters that may indicate replication issues.

6. Replication Notifications:
- Enable replication notifications on DCs to receive alerts when replication issues occur.
- Notifications can help you proactively address replication problems before they escalate.

7. Regular Health Checks:
- Perform regular health checks of AD replication using tools like Repadmin and ADREPLSTATUS.
- Schedule regular checks to ensure that replication is functioning correctly.

8. Review Replication Schedule:
- Review the replication schedule for site links in Active Directory Sites and Services.
- Ensure that replication schedules are configured appropriately for your environment.

9. Review DNS Configuration:
- Regularly review and verify the DNS configuration for DCs to ensure proper name resolution.
- DNS issues can impact replication, so it's important to address any DNS-related problems.

10. Monitor Network Connectivity:
- Monitor network connectivity between DCs to ensure that there are no issues that may impact replication.
- Use network monitoring tools to detect and resolve connectivity problems.

By regularly monitoring replication health using these methods, you can ensure that changes are replicated correctly and efficiently in your Active Directory environment, helping to maintain its integrity and reliability.

ISSO-TECH

VICTOR P HENDERSON | ISSO-TECH ENTERPRISES™
CERTIFIED ETHICAL HACKER C|EH

ISSO-TECH PRESS™

CHAPTER 14
DNS
IMPLEMENTATION

CHAPTER 14: DNS IMPLEMENTATION
ACTIVE DIRECTORY INTEGRATION

- DNS requirements for Active Directory
DNS (Domain Name System) is a fundamental component of Active Directory (AD) and plays a crucial role in its operation. Here are the key DNS requirements for Active Directory:

1. Domain Name Resolution:
- DNS is used for resolving domain names to IP addresses.
- AD requires that all domain-joined machines, including domain controllers, use DNS for name resolution.

2. SRV Records:
- AD uses SRV (Service) records in DNS to locate domain controllers for authentication and other services.
- SRV records are critical for clients to locate domain controllers and other AD-related services.

3. Domain Name Structure:
- AD domain names should be registered DNS names (e.g., contoso.com).
- Internal AD domain names should not be single-label names (e.g., "example" instead of "example.local").

4. Dynamic DNS Updates:
- AD-integrated DNS zones support dynamic updates, allowing DNS records to be automatically updated as AD changes occur.
- Dynamic DNS updates are crucial for maintaining accurate and up-to-date DNS records.

ISSO-TECH PRESS™

5. Forward and Reverse Lookup Zones:

- AD requires both forward (name-to-IP) and reverse (IP-to-name) lookup zones to function properly.
- Reverse lookup zones are particularly important for AD-related services, such as Kerberos authentication.

6. Secure Dynamic Updates:

- Secure dynamic updates ensure that only authorized clients can update DNS records.
- This helps prevent unauthorized changes to DNS records, which could compromise AD security.

7. Global Catalog (GC) Locator DNS Records:

- AD requires DNS records for locating global catalog servers, which are important for cross-domain authentication and searching.
- These records are used by clients to locate a global catalog server in the forest.

8. Root Hints and Forwarders:

- DNS servers in an AD environment should be configured with root hints or forwarders to resolve external DNS queries.
- This ensures that DNS queries for external domains are resolved correctly.

9. Replication:

- DNS data is replicated between DNS servers in an AD-integrated DNS zone.
- AD replication relies on DNS replication for proper functioning.

10. Scalability and Performance:

- DNS servers in an AD environment should be scalable and able to handle the DNS query load generated by AD clients and services.
- Proper DNS server configuration and optimization can improve AD performance.

11. Fault Tolerance:

- AD requires fault-tolerant DNS infrastructure to ensure that DNS services remain available even in the event of a DNS server failure.
- Use of multiple DNS servers and DNS zone replication can help achieve fault tolerance.

By meeting these DNS requirements, you can ensure that Active Directory operates smoothly and reliably, providing essential services to your organization's infrastructure.

- Diagnosing DNS-related issues
Diagnosing DNS-related issues in an Active Directory (AD) environment is crucial for maintaining proper functionality. Here's a step-by-step guide to diagnosing DNS problems:

1. Check DNS Server Configuration:

- Ensure that the DNS server's IP address is correctly configured on the client machine.
- Verify that the DNS server is reachable from the client by using the "ping" command.

2. Check DNS Server Status:

- Verify that the DNS server is running and accepting queries.
- Check the DNS server's event logs for any errors or warnings.

3. Verify DNS Records:

- Check the DNS records for the domain controller (DC) and other AD-related services (e.g., Global Catalog) using the "nslookup" command.
- Ensure that the correct DNS records (e.g., A, AAAA, SRV) exist for the DCs and that they resolve correctly.

4. Check DNS Zone Configuration:

- Verify that the DNS zone configuration, including forward and reverse lookup zones, is correct.
- Check for any misconfigured or missing DNS zones.

5. Check DNS Replication:

- Ensure that DNS zone data is being replicated correctly between DNS servers in an AD-integrated zone.
- Use the "dnscmd" command to check the status of DNS replication.

6. Check DNS Client Settings:

- Verify that the client machines are configured to use the correct DNS server.
- Check the DNS suffix search list and ensure it is configured correctly.

7. Test DNS Resolution:

- Use the "nslookup" command to test DNS resolution for domain names and IP addresses.
- Verify that both forward and reverse lookups are working correctly.

8. Check for DNS Forwarding or Root Hints Issues:

- If DNS forwarding or root hints are used, ensure that they are configured correctly.
- Check the DNS server's forwarders or root hints configuration for any misconfigurations.

9. Check Firewall Settings:

- Ensure that there are no firewall rules blocking DNS traffic between clients and DNS servers.
- Check the DNS server's firewall settings to allow DNS traffic.

10. Check DNS Cache:

- If DNS caching is enabled, clear the DNS cache on the client and DNS server to ensure that stale entries are not causing issues.

11. Review DNS Event Logs:

- Check the DNS server's event logs for any DNS-related errors or warnings that may indicate a problem.
- Look for event IDs related to DNS server startup, zone loading, and DNS queries.

By following these steps, you can diagnose and resolve DNS-related issues in an AD environment, ensuring that DNS services operate smoothly and efficiently.
- Best practices for DNS and Active Directory integration
Integrating DNS with Active Directory (AD) is crucial for AD's operation, as AD heavily relies on DNS for name resolution and service location. Here are some best practices for DNS and AD integration:

1. Use AD-Integrated Zones:
- Store DNS zones in AD-integrated zones to leverage AD's security and replication features.
- AD-integrated zones replicate DNS data along with AD data, ensuring consistency and reducing administrative overhead.

2. DNS Server Placement:
- Place DNS servers on domain controllers (DCs) to provide both AD and DNS services from the same server.
- Distribute DNS servers across different AD sites for fault tolerance and to reduce network latency for name resolution.

3. Forwarders and Root Hints:
- Use DNS forwarders or root hints to resolve external DNS queries for which the DNS server is not authoritative.
- Configure forwarders to point to external DNS servers provided by your ISP or a public DNS service like Google DNS or OpenDNS.

4. Secure Dynamic Updates:
- Enable secure dynamic updates for AD-integrated zones to ensure that only authorized clients can update DNS records.
- This helps prevent unauthorized changes to DNS records and protects against DNS spoofing attacks.

5. DNS Scavenging:
- Enable DNS scavenging to remove stale DNS records from the DNS database.
- This helps keep the DNS database clean and reduces the risk of name resolution issues due to outdated records.

@ISSO.TECH.ENTERPRISES

6. Name Resolution Order:

- Configure the DNS client settings on computers to prioritize AD DNS servers for name resolution.
- This ensures that AD-related queries are resolved by AD DNS servers first, reducing the likelihood of issues related to incorrect or outdated DNS records.

7. DNS Forward Lookup Zones:

- Use forward lookup zones to map hostnames to IP addresses for name resolution.
- Ensure that forward lookup zones are properly configured and contain the necessary DNS records for AD services and resources.

8. Reverse Lookup Zones:

- Use reverse lookup zones to map IP addresses to hostnames for reverse name resolution.
- Ensure that reverse lookup zones are properly configured and contain PTR records for all IP addresses in use in the network.

9. Monitoring and Maintenance:

- Regularly monitor DNS server performance and availability.
- Perform routine maintenance tasks, such as checking DNS logs for errors, monitoring DNS replication, and reviewing DNS zone configurations.

10. Backup and Restore:

- Implement a backup strategy for DNS data to ensure that DNS zones and records can be restored in case of data loss or corruption.
- Regularly test the backup and restore process to ensure its effectiveness.

Following these best practices helps ensure that DNS and AD integration is reliable, secure, and efficient, providing a solid foundation for your organization's IT infrastructure.

@ISSO.TECH.ENTERPRISES

ISSO-TECH

VICTOR P HENDERSON | ISSO-TECH ENTERPRISES™
CERTIFIED ETHICAL HACKER C|EH

ISSO-TECH PRESS™

CHAPTER 15
GROUP POLICY

CHAPTER 15: GROUP POLICY
SECURING ACTIVE DIRECTORY

Overview of Group Policy

Group Policy is a feature in Microsoft Windows that allows administrators to manage the settings of users and computers in an Active Directory environment. It provides centralized management and configuration of operating systems, applications, and user settings. Here is an overview of Group Policy:

1. Scope:
- Group Policy settings can be applied at the domain, site, or organizational unit (OU) level in Active Directory.
- Policies applied at higher levels in the hierarchy can be overridden by policies applied at lower levels.

2. Group Policy Objects (GPOs):
- A Group Policy Object (GPO) is a collection of settings that define how a system should behave for a group of users or computers.
- GPOs are stored in Active Directory and can be linked to domains, sites, or OUs.

3. Settings:
- Group Policy settings can be used to configure a wide range of options, including security settings, desktop settings, application settings, and more.
- Settings can be applied to control access to resources, enforce security policies, configure user environments, and manage software installations.

4. Management:
- Group Policy settings are managed using the Group Policy Management Console (GPMC), which provides a graphical interface for creating, editing, and managing GPOs.
- GPMC allows administrators to delegate control of GPOs to specific users or groups.

5. Processing:
- Group Policy settings are processed in a specific order: Local Group Policy, Site, Domain, Organizational Unit.
- Settings from higher-level GPOs are processed first, followed by settings from lower-level GPOs, allowing for inheritance and overriding of settings.

6. Filtering:
- Group Policy settings can be filtered based on security group membership, user or computer characteristics, or other criteria.
- This allows administrators to apply specific settings to different groups of users or computers within the same OU.

7. Security:
- Group Policy settings can be used to enforce security policies, such as password policies, account lockout policies, and user rights assignment.
- Settings can also be used to configure Windows Firewall settings, BitLocker encryption, and other security-related features.

8. Troubleshooting:
- Group Policy modeling and results tools can be used to troubleshoot Group Policy processing and determine which settings are applied to a specific user or computer.

@ISSO.TECH.ENTERPRISES

- Event logs and the Resultant Set of Policy (RSoP) tool can also be used to diagnose and resolve Group Policy-related issues.
Group Policy is a powerful tool for managing and configuring Windows environments, providing administrators with granular control over system settings and configurations.

- Troubleshooting Group Policy application
Troubleshooting Group Policy application involves identifying and resolving issues that prevent Group Policy settings from being applied correctly to users or computers in an Active Directory environment. Here are some common troubleshooting steps:

1. Check Group Policy Objects (GPOs):
- Ensure that the GPOs containing the desired settings are linked to the correct Organizational Units (OUs), domains, or sites.
- Verify that the GPOs are enabled and have the correct security filtering and delegation settings.

2. Check Group Policy Inheritance:
- Ensure that there are no conflicting GPOs that may be overriding the desired settings.
- Use the Resultant Set of Policy (RSoP) tool to view the applied GPOs and settings for a specific user or computer.

3. Check Group Policy Processing:
- Use the Group Policy Modeling and Group Policy Results tools to simulate and analyze Group Policy processing for a specific user or computer.
- Check the event logs on the client and domain controller for any Group Policy-related errors or warnings.

ISSO-TECH PRESS™

4. Check User and Computer Membership:

- Verify that the user or computer is in the correct OU or security group to which the GPO is linked.
- Ensure that there are no issues with Active Directory replication that may affect group membership.

5. Check Network Connectivity:

- Ensure that the client can communicate with the domain controller and access the SYSVOL share where Group Policy settings are stored.
- Check for any network issues, such as DNS resolution problems or firewall blocking Group Policy traffic.

6. Check Group Policy Permissions:

- Verify that the user or computer has Read and Apply Group Policy permissions on the GPOs containing the desired settings.
- Check for any issues with security filtering or delegation that may prevent the GPOs from being applied.

7. Check WMI Filters:

- If GPOs are using WMI filters, ensure that the WMI filters are correctly configured and are evaluating to true for the target user or computer.

8. Check Group Policy Preferences:

- If GPOs are using Group Policy Preferences, ensure that the client has the necessary Group Policy Preference Client Side Extensions installed.
- Check for any issues with Group Policy Preference item-level targeting that may affect the application of settings.

9. Force Group Policy Update:

- Use the "gpupdate" command on the client to force a Group Policy update.
- Use the "gpupdate /force" command to force a complete Group Policy update, including reapplying all settings.

10. Restart the Client:

- Sometimes, a simple restart of the client computer is all that is needed to apply Group Policy settings correctly.

By following these troubleshooting steps, you can identify and resolve issues that prevent Group Policy settings from being applied correctly, ensuring that users and computers receive the intended configurations and settings.

- Best practices for Group Policy management

Managing Group Policy effectively is crucial for maintaining a secure and well-managed Windows environment. Here are some best practices for Group Policy management:

1. Plan and Organize GPOs:

- Use a logical and organized structure for GPOs, grouping them based on their purpose or target audience.
- Avoid creating overly complex GPOs with too many settings, as this can make troubleshooting and maintenance difficult.

2. Use Security Filtering Wisely:

- Use security filtering to target GPOs to specific users or computers based on security group membership.
- Avoid using individual user or computer accounts for security filtering, as this can lead to complexity and potential security issues.

3. Avoid Overlapping GPOs:

- Ensure that GPOs do not overlap in their settings, as conflicting settings can lead to unpredictable behavior.
- Use the Resultant Set of Policy (RSoP) tool to analyze the combined effect of GPOs on a user or computer.

4. Regularly Review and Clean Up GPOs:

- Periodically review GPOs to ensure they are still necessary and relevant.
- Remove any unused or obsolete GPOs to reduce complexity and improve performance.

5. Delegate GPO Management:

- Delegate GPO management tasks to specific administrators or groups using the Delegation tab in the Group Policy Management Console (GPMC).
- Use caution when delegating permissions to ensure that only authorized personnel have access to GPOs.

6. Use GPO Backups:

- Regularly back up GPOs using the Group Policy Management Console (GPMC) or PowerShell.
- Store GPO backups in a secure location to ensure they are available for recovery if needed.

7. Document GPO Settings:

- Maintain documentation of GPO settings, including the purpose of the GPO, the settings applied, and any exceptions or special configurations.
- Documenting GPO settings can help with troubleshooting and auditing.

@ISSO.TECH.ENTERPRISES

8. Test GPOs Before Deployment:
- Use a test environment to validate GPO settings before deploying them to production.
- Test GPOs with a representative sample of users and computers to ensure they behave as expected.

9. Monitor GPO Application:
- Monitor the application of GPOs using tools like Group Policy Results (gpresult) or Group Policy Modeling in the Group Policy Management Console (GPMC).
- Regularly review the event logs on clients and domain controllers for any Group Policy-related errors or warnings.

10. Stay Informed about Group Policy Changes:
- Keep up to date with changes and updates to Group Policy, including new features and best practices.
- Subscribe to Microsoft's Group Policy blog and other relevant resources for the latest information.

By following these best practices, you can effectively manage Group Policy in your organization, ensuring that it remains a reliable and secure tool for configuring and managing Windows environments.

ISSO-TECH

VICTOR P HENDERSON | ISSO-TECH ENTERPRISES™
CERTIFIED ETHICAL HACKER C|EH

ISSO-TECH PRESS™

CHAPTER 16
AD DATABASE ADMINISTRATION

CHAPTER 16 | AD DATABASE ADMINISTRATION
MAINTENANCE AND MONITORING

Monitoring and maintaining the Active Directory database
Monitoring and maintaining the Active Directory (AD) database is crucial for ensuring the health and performance of your AD environment. Here are some best practices for monitoring and maintaining the AD database:

1. Monitoring Tools:
- Use monitoring tools such as Performance Monitor (Perfmon), Event Viewer, and AD Replication Status Tool to monitor the health and performance of AD.
- Third-party monitoring tools can also provide more advanced monitoring capabilities.

2. Regular Backups:
- Regularly back up the AD database and system state using Windows Server Backup or third-party backup solutions.
- Store backups in a secure location and test the restore process regularly to ensure data recoverability.

3. Database Integrity Checks:
- Use the "ntdsutil" command to perform regular integrity checks on the AD database.
- Monitor the Directory Services event log for events related to database integrity.

4. Performance Tuning:
- Monitor AD performance metrics such as CPU usage, memory usage, disk I/O, and replication latency.

- Use tools like Performance Monitor (Perfmon) to identify and address performance bottlenecks.

5. Database Maintenance:
- Regularly defragment the AD database using the "ntdsutil" command to improve database performance.
- Monitor the Directory Services event log for events related to database maintenance.

6. Monitoring Replication:
- Monitor AD replication using tools like Repadmin and AD Replication Status Tool to ensure replication is healthy.
- Monitor the Directory Services event log for events related to replication.

7. Security Monitoring:
- Monitor AD for security events using tools like Event Viewer and Security Configuration and Analysis.
- Enable auditing of AD objects and monitor for suspicious activity.

8. Patch Management:
- Regularly apply Windows updates and patches to servers hosting AD to protect against security vulnerabilities.
- Test patches in a non-production environment before applying them to production servers.

9. Capacity Planning:
- Monitor AD database size and plan for future growth.
- Consider implementing quotas and cleanup policies for objects to prevent database bloat.

@ISSO.TECH.ENTERPRISES

10. Regular Health Checks:

- Perform regular health checks of AD using tools like Microsoft's Best Practices Analyzer (BPA) to identify and address issues.
- Review AD configuration and settings to ensure they align with best practices and security standards.

By following these best practices, you can ensure that your AD database remains healthy, secure, and performant, providing a reliable foundation for your organization's IT infrastructure.

- Performing database integrity checks

Performing database integrity checks on the Active Directory (AD) database is important for ensuring its health and reliability. Here's how you can perform database integrity checks:

1. Open Command Prompt:

- On a domain controller, open Command Prompt as an administrator.

2. Enter NTDSUTIL:

- Type `ntdsutil` and press Enter to launch the NTDSUTIL utility.

3. Activate the Database Maintenance Mode:

- Type `activate instance ntds` and press Enter to activate the database maintenance mode.

4. Run Integrity Check:

- Type `integrity` and press Enter to start the integrity check.

5. Check Database Integrity:

- Type `files` and press Enter to check the database integrity.

VICTOR P HENDERSON | ISSO-TECH ENTERPRISES™
CERTIFIED ETHICAL HACKER C|EH

ISSO-TECH PRESS™

229.320.151.8

6. Exit NTDSUTIL:
- Type `q` and press Enter to exit the NTDSUTIL utility.

7. Restart Domain Controller:
- Restart the domain controller to exit the database maintenance mode.
Performing regular database integrity checks helps ensure that the AD database is free from corruption and maintains optimal performance.

- Optimizing the Active Directory database
Optimizing the Active Directory (AD) database is important for maintaining its performance and efficiency. Here are some steps to optimize the AD database:

1. Regular Database Maintenance:
- Perform regular database maintenance tasks, such as defragmentation, to optimize the database structure and improve performance.
- Use the `ntdsutil` utility to perform offline defragmentation of the AD database.

2. Monitor Performance Metrics:
- Monitor performance metrics, such as CPU usage, memory usage, disk I/O, and replication latency, to identify areas for optimization.
- Use tools like Performance Monitor (Perfmon) to track these metrics over time.

@ISSO.TECH.ENTERPRISES

3. Review AD Configuration:
- Review the AD configuration, including site topology, replication settings, and group policies, to ensure they are optimized for performance.
- Make adjustments as needed to improve performance.

4. Monitor and Tune Indexes:
- Monitor the performance of AD indexes and tune them as needed to improve query performance.
- Use tools like the Active Directory Performance Testing Tool (ADTest) to analyze index performance.

5. Optimize Replication:
- Optimize AD replication by ensuring that replication is occurring efficiently and without unnecessary delays.
- Monitor replication traffic and adjust replication schedules as needed to optimize performance.

6. Remove Unused or Obsolete Objects:
- Regularly remove unused or obsolete objects from the AD database to reduce database size and improve performance.
- Use tools like AD Cleanup Wizard or PowerShell scripts to identify and remove these objects.

7. Regular Backups:
- Regularly back up the AD database and system state to protect against data loss and corruption.
- Test the restore process to ensure backups are viable.

8. Implement Monitoring and Alerting:

- Implement monitoring and alerting for AD performance metrics to quickly identify and address performance issues.
- Use tools like System Center Operations Manager (SCOM) or third-party monitoring tools for this purpose.

9. Consider Hardware Upgrades:

- Consider upgrading hardware, such as adding more RAM or faster disks, to improve AD performance if software optimizations are not sufficient.

10. Review and Optimize Group Policies:

- Review and optimize Group Policies to reduce the number of policies applied and simplify policy settings.
- Use tools like Group Policy Management Console (GPMC) to analyze and optimize Group Policy settings.

By following these steps, you can optimize the Active Directory database for better performance and reliability.

@ISSO.TECH.ENTERPRISES

ACTIVE DIRECTORY MIGRATION STRATEGIES

Planning for Migration

Effective planning is a crucial component of any successful Active Directory (AD) migration project. Small businesses, IT professionals, network engineers, and system engineers must approach the migration process with a comprehensive strategy that takes into account the unique requirements and limitations of their environment. The first step in this planning phase is to assess the current AD infrastructure. This involves a thorough inventory of existing users, groups, organizational units (OUs), and resources. Understanding the existing structure not only aids in determining what needs to be migrated but also helps identify potential security risks and compliance issues that may arise during the transition.

Once the current environment has been assessed, the next critical step is defining the scope and objectives of the migration. Clearly articulated goals will serve as a guiding light throughout the process. Businesses must determine whether they are moving to a new on-premises AD setup, transitioning to a cloud-based environment such as Azure AD, or implementing a hybrid approach. Each option presents its own set of challenges and advantages, particularly in terms of Active Directory security best practices. Ensuring that the new environment adheres to established security protocols is paramount, as it protects sensitive information and maintains compliance with industry regulations.

An essential aspect of planning for migration is the development of a detailed migration strategy. This strategy should outline the steps involved in the migration process, including timelines, resource allocation, and responsibilities. IT professionals should consider the use of PowerShell automation to streamline repetitive tasks, such as user account creation and group policy migration. Leveraging PowerShell scripts can significantly reduce the likelihood of human error while enhancing the overall efficiency of the migration. Additionally, it is important to establish a rollback plan to address any unforeseen issues that may arise during the migration.

Testing the migration plan is a vital step that should not be overlooked. Before executing the migration in a live environment, conducting a pilot migration can help identify potential pitfalls and refine the strategy. This phase should include thorough testing of user authentication protocols and group policies to ensure that they function as intended in the new environment. Engaging in this level of testing not only mitigates risks but also fosters confidence among stakeholders in the migration process. Documenting the results of the pilot migration will provide valuable insights that can be applied to the full-scale rollout.

Finally, communication plays a pivotal role in the success of an Active Directory migration. Keeping all stakeholders informed about the migration plan, timelines, and potential impact on operations is essential for managing expectations. Training sessions for end-users and IT staff can facilitate a smoother transition, as individuals become familiar with any new processes or tools being introduced. An effective migration strategy not only enhances operational efficiency but also positions small businesses to leverage the advantages of modern Active Directory capabilities,

@ISSO.TECH.ENTERPRISES

such as improved security, streamlined management, and enhanced integration with cloud services.

Executing Migration Projects

Migrating Active Directory (AD) environments is a multifaceted process that demands careful planning and execution to ensure minimal disruption to business operations. For small businesses and IT professionals, the stakes are particularly high, as the success of these migrations can directly impact productivity and security. This chapter outlines a structured approach to executing migration projects, emphasizing the importance of assessing current environments, defining migration strategies, leveraging automation tools like PowerShell, and implementing best practices to safeguard against potential disruptions.

The first step in any migration project involves conducting a thorough assessment of the existing Active Directory environment. This includes evaluating the current infrastructure, identifying dependencies, and determining the overall health of the AD setup. Small businesses often have limited resources, making it essential to prioritize critical components that must be preserved or improved during the migration. Tools such as PowerShell can facilitate comprehensive health checks and reporting, enabling IT professionals to pinpoint issues and gather the necessary intelligence to inform their migration strategy.

Once the assessment is complete, defining a clear migration strategy is crucial. This strategy should outline the objectives, scope, and timeline for the migration. Key considerations include the choice between a phased migration, which allows for gradual transitions, or a cutover approach, which may be more suitable for organizations requiring a complete switch within a short timeframe. It is vital to involve stakeholders throughout this process to ensure that the migration aligns with business goals and minimizes operational disruptions.

Automation plays a pivotal role in executing migration projects effectively. PowerShell, a powerful scripting language, can streamline repetitive tasks, reduce human error, and enhance efficiency. IT professionals can use PowerShell scripts to automate user account migrations, group policy transfers, and permissions adjustments, thereby accelerating the overall process. Moreover, automating backup procedures during the migration phase can provide an essential safety net, allowing for quick recovery in the event of unforeseen complications.

Finally, implementing best practices during the migration execution is crucial for achieving a smooth transition. This includes thorough testing of the new environment before going live, ensuring robust security measures are in place, and maintaining clear communication with all stakeholders. Additionally, establishing a rollback plan will provide a contingency option should critical issues arise post-migration. By adhering to these principles, small businesses and IT professionals can navigate the complexities of Active Directory migrations effectively, ultimately leading to improved operational efficiency and enhanced security in their IT environments.

Post-Migration Best Practices

Post-migration best practices are essential for ensuring a smooth transition and ongoing efficiency after migrating Active Directory (AD) tasks with PowerShell. For small businesses and IT professionals, understanding these practices can significantly enhance the security, reliability, and performance of their Active Directory environments. This subchapter will outline key strategies to adopt post-migration, focusing on monitoring, optimization, documentation, security, and training.

First and foremost, continuous monitoring is a critical practice that should be implemented immediately following migration. Utilizing PowerShell scripts to track performance metrics, user activity, and system health can help identify potential issues before they escalate. By establishing automated alerts for unusual activity or performance degradation, IT professionals can ensure that any anomalies are addressed promptly. Regular audits of logs and reports will facilitate an understanding of the environment's behavior and provide insights into areas that may require further optimization.

Optimization should also be a priority after migration. This involves reviewing and fine-tuning Group Policies, user permissions, and access controls to align with the organization's operational needs. Leveraging PowerShell for bulk modifications and adjustments can streamline this process. Additionally, evaluating the replication topology and ensuring that domain controllers are efficiently communicating can prevent latency issues and ensure that changes propagate seamlessly across the network. Such optimizations not only enhance performance but also contribute to a more secure and manageable Active Directory environment.

Documentation is another vital best practice that cannot be overlooked. Comprehensive documentation of the migration process, including any custom scripts and configurations, serves as a valuable resource for troubleshooting and future migrations. Maintaining up-to-date records of all changes made during the migration helps in compliance audits and ensures that both current and future IT staff have access to critical information. Furthermore, establishing a knowledge base that outlines best practices and common troubleshooting steps can expedite issue resolution and enhance overall team productivity.

Security must remain a top priority in the post-migration phase. Implementing advanced security measures, such as multi-factor authentication and regular password audits, can help safeguard against unauthorized access. PowerShell can be used to automate security updates and compliance checks, reinforcing the importance of adhering to security best practices. Regularly reviewing permissions and access controls, along with conducting penetration testing, will help identify vulnerabilities and mitigate risks, ensuring that the Active Directory environment remains robust against potential threats.

Lastly, investing in training and professional development is essential for IT staff involved with Active Directory management. Providing ongoing education about the latest PowerShell functionalities, security practices, and troubleshooting techniques equips professionals with the skills necessary to manage an

@ISSO.TECH.ENTERPRISES

evolving IT landscape effectively. Encouraging team members to take advantage of available resources, such as online courses and user communities, fosters a culture of continuous improvement. By prioritizing these post-migration best practices, small businesses can ensure that their Active Directory environments are not only functional but also optimized for future growth and security.

ISSO-TECH

VICTOR P HENDERSON | ISSO-TECH ENTERPRISES™
CERTIFIED ETHICAL HACKER C|EH

ISSO-TECH PRESS™

229.320.151.8

CHAPTER 17
WINDOWS SERVER

CHAPTER 17 | WINDOWS SERVER
DISASTER RECOVERY AND BACKUP

Backup and recovery strategies for Active Directory

Implementing a robust backup and recovery strategy for Active Directory (AD) is crucial for ensuring business continuity and data protection. Here are some best practices for backup and recovery of AD:

1. Regular Backups:

- Schedule regular backups of the AD database and system state using Windows Server Backup, third-party backup solutions, or cloud-based backup services.
- Back up all domain controllers in the domain to ensure redundancy.

2. System State Backup:

- Ensure that the system state backup includes critical AD components, such as the AD database, SYSVOL folder, and the registry.
- The system state backup is essential for recovering AD in case of a disaster.

3. Backup Retention:

- Define a backup retention policy to determine how long backups should be retained.
- Consider regulatory and compliance requirements when defining the retention policy.

4. Offsite Backup Storage:

- Store backups in an offsite location to protect against on-premises disasters, such as fire, flood, or theft.

VICTOR P HENDERSON | ISSO-TECH ENTERPRISES™
CERTIFIED ETHICAL HACKER C|EH

ISSO-TECH PRESS™

229.320.151.8

- Use encrypted backups to ensure data security during transit and storage.

5. Test Backups:

- Regularly test backups to ensure they are valid and can be restored successfully.
- Perform test restores in a non-production environment to verify the integrity of backups.

6. Document Backup Procedures:

- Document backup procedures, including schedules, retention policies, and restore processes.
- Ensure that all IT staff responsible for backup and recovery are familiar with these procedures.

7. Automate Backup Tasks:

- Use automation tools to schedule and manage backup tasks, ensuring consistency and reliability.
- Automate notifications for backup successes and failures to promptly address any issues.

8. Implement Monitoring:

- Monitor backup processes and logs to ensure that backups are completing successfully.
- Implement alerts for backup failures or issues that require attention.

9. Disaster Recovery Plan:

- Develop a comprehensive disaster recovery plan that includes procedures for recovering AD in various scenarios, such as hardware failure, data corruption, or cyberattacks.

© **MASTERING ACTIVE DIRECTORY**

@ISSO.TECH.ENTERPRISES

- Test the disaster recovery plan regularly to ensure its effectiveness.

10. Consider Virtualization:
- If your AD infrastructure is virtualized, leverage virtualization-specific backup solutions that can perform efficient backups and granular restores of AD.

By following these best practices, you can ensure that your AD environment is well-protected and can be recovered quickly in the event of a disaster or data loss.

- Performing authoritative and non-authoritative restores
Performing authoritative and non-authoritative restores are essential tasks in Active Directory (AD) recovery scenarios. Here's an overview of these processes:

1. Non-Authoritative Restore:
- A non-authoritative restore is used when you want to restore the AD database to a previous state without affecting the current state of the domain.
- During a non-authoritative restore, the AD database is restored from a backup, and then AD replication updates the restored database with changes from other domain controllers.
Steps to perform a non-authoritative restore:
- Boot into Directory Services Restore Mode (DSRM) on the domain controller.
- Restore the system state or AD database from backup using Windows Server Backup or another backup solution.
- Restart the domain controller normally, and AD replication will update the restored database with changes from other domain controllers.

2. Authoritative Restore:

- An authoritative restore is used when you want to restore a specific object or set of objects in AD to a previous state and make sure that those objects replicate to all other domain controllers.
- After an authoritative restore, the restored objects are marked as authoritative, and AD replication ensures that these objects are replicated to all other domain controllers.
Steps to perform an authoritative restore:
- Perform a non-authoritative restore as described above.
- Use the ntdsutil command-line tool to mark the objects as authoritative.
- Restart the domain controller in normal mode, and AD replication will replicate the authoritative objects to all other domain controllers.
It's important to note that authoritative restores should be used with caution, as restoring objects as authoritative can potentially overwrite newer changes made to those objects in the AD database. Always ensure you have a valid backup and a well-documented recovery plan before performing any restore operations in AD.
- Planning for disaster recovery scenarios

Planning for disaster recovery (DR) scenarios in Active Directory (AD) is crucial for ensuring business continuity and data protection. Here's a comprehensive approach to planning for DR in AD:

1. Risk Assessment:

- Identify potential risks and threats to your AD environment, such as hardware failure, data corruption, natural disasters, or cyberattacks.
- Assess the impact of these risks on your organization's operations and prioritize them based on their likelihood and severity.

@ISSO.TECH.ENTERPRISES

2. Define Recovery Objectives:
- Define recovery time objectives (RTOs) and recovery point objectives (RPOs) for AD.
- RTO defines the maximum acceptable downtime for AD services, while RPO defines the maximum acceptable data loss.

3. Backup Strategy:
- Implement a robust backup strategy for AD, including regular backups of the AD database and system state.
- Ensure backups are stored securely and can be accessed in the event of a disaster.

4. Replication Strategy:
- Use AD replication to replicate AD data to multiple domain controllers in different locations.
- Ensure that replication is configured properly and monitor its health regularly.

5. Test Restore Procedures:
- Regularly test restore procedures to ensure that backups can be restored successfully in the event of a disaster.
- Perform test restores in a non-production environment to validate the integrity of backups.

6. Disaster Recovery Plan:
- Develop a comprehensive disaster recovery plan that includes procedures for recovering AD in various scenarios, such as hardware failure, data corruption, or cyberattacks.
- Define roles and responsibilities for DR team members and ensure they are trained on the DR plan.

7. Communication Plan:
- Develop a communication plan to notify stakeholders, employees, and customers in the event of a disaster.
- Include contact information for key personnel and emergency services.

8. DR Testing:
- Regularly test the DR plan to ensure its effectiveness.
- Conduct tabletop exercises and simulations to test the DR plan without disrupting production systems.

9. Monitoring and Auditing:
- Implement monitoring and auditing tools to monitor the health and performance of AD.
- Monitor for any signs of potential issues or vulnerabilities that could lead to a disaster.

10. Documentation and Reporting:
- Document all aspects of the DR plan, including procedures, contact information, and recovery strategies.
- Generate regular reports on the status of the DR plan and any updates or changes made to it.

By following these steps, you can ensure that your organization is prepared to recover from a disaster and minimize the impact on your operations.

ISSO-TECH

VICTOR P HENDERSON | ISSO-TECH ENTERPRISES™
CERTIFIED ETHICAL HACKER C|EH

ISSO-TECH PRESS™

CHAPTER 18
SECURITY & AUDITING

CHAPTER 18: SECURITY AND AUDITING
TRACKING CHANGES

Auditing Active Directory changes
Auditing changes in Active Directory (AD) is crucial for maintaining security, compliance, and accountability. Here's how you can audit AD changes:

1. Enable Auditing:
- Enable auditing of AD changes by configuring the appropriate audit policies in Group Policy.
- Use the "Advanced Audit Policy Configuration" settings to enable more granular auditing of specific events.

2. Configure Auditing Settings:
- Configure auditing settings to track changes to objects, such as users, groups, computers, and organizational units (OUs).
- Enable auditing for both successful and failed events to capture all relevant changes.

3. Use Windows Event Viewer:
- Use the Windows Event Viewer to view and analyze audit events related to AD changes.
- Look for events with event IDs such as 5136 (AD object modified), 5137 (AD object created), and 5141 (AD object deleted).

4. Enable Object Access Auditing:
- Enable Object Access auditing to track access to AD objects, such as files, folders, and registry keys.
- This can help you identify unauthorized access attempts to sensitive AD data.

VICTOR P HENDERSON | ISSO-TECH ENTERPRISES™
CERTIFIED ETHICAL HACKER C|EH

ISSO-TECH PRESS™

5. Review Audit Logs Regularly:

- Regularly review audit logs to identify and investigate unauthorized or suspicious changes in AD.
- Use filtering and sorting options in Event Viewer to focus on specific types of events or time periods.

6. Use Third-Party Tools:

- Consider using third-party auditing tools that provide more advanced features and reporting capabilities.
- These tools can help automate the auditing process and provide more detailed insights into AD changes.

7. Monitor Active Directory Replication:

- Monitor AD replication to ensure that audit logs are replicated to all domain controllers.
- This ensures that audit data is not lost in the event of a domain controller failure.

8. Implement Change Management Processes:

- Implement change management processes to track and approve changes to AD objects.
- This can help prevent unauthorized changes and ensure accountability for all changes made in AD.

By following these best practices, you can effectively audit changes in Active Directory and ensure the security and integrity of your AD environment.

- Detecting and responding to security threats
Detecting and responding to security threats in Active Directory (AD) is crucial for protecting your organization's data and resources.

@ISSO.TECH.ENTERPRISES

Here are some best practices for detecting and responding to security threats in AD:

1. Enable Auditing:
- Enable auditing of critical AD events, such as changes to user accounts, group memberships, and administrative activity.
- Use tools like Windows Event Viewer or third-party solutions to monitor and analyze audit logs for suspicious activity.

2. Monitor Account Activity:
- Monitor account activity, such as logins, failed logins, and account lockouts, to detect unauthorized access attempts.
- Use tools like Microsoft Advanced Threat Analytics (ATA) or Azure Advanced Threat Protection (ATP) for real-time monitoring of account activity.

3. Implement Security Monitoring:
- Use intrusion detection systems (IDS) and intrusion prevention systems (IPS) to monitor network traffic for signs of malicious activity.
- Implement endpoint detection and response (EDR) solutions to monitor endpoints for suspicious behavior.

4. Enable Security Logging:
- Enable security logging on domain controllers and other critical servers to capture detailed information about security-related events.
- Use tools like Sysmon to enhance logging capabilities and capture additional security-related data.

5. Implement Security Policies:
- Implement security policies that restrict user privileges, enforce strong password policies, and limit access to sensitive resources.
- Regularly review and update security policies to address emerging threats.

6. Perform Regular Security Audits:
- Conduct regular security audits of AD to identify vulnerabilities and misconfigurations.
- Use tools like Microsoft Baseline Security Analyzer (MBSA) or PowerShell scripts to automate security audits.

7. Respond to Incidents:
- Develop and implement an incident response plan to quickly respond to security incidents.
- Define roles and responsibilities for incident response team members and establish communication channels for reporting and escalating incidents.

8. Educate Users:
- Educate users about security best practices, such as recognizing phishing attacks and avoiding suspicious links and attachments.
- Conduct regular security awareness training to keep users informed about the latest threats.

9. Patch Management:
- Regularly apply security patches and updates to AD servers, domain controllers, and other critical systems.
- Use automated patch management tools to streamline the patching process and ensure timely deployment of patches.

@ISSO.TECH.ENTERPRISES

By following these best practices, you can improve your organization's ability to detect and respond to security threats in Active Directory, reducing the risk of data breaches and unauthorized access.

- Implementing security best practices
Implementing security best practices in Active Directory (AD) is essential for protecting your organization's data and infrastructure. Here are some key security best practices for AD:

1. Use Strong Passwords:
- Enforce strong password policies, including minimum length, complexity, and expiration requirements.
- Consider implementing multi-factor authentication (MFA) for added security.

2. Limit Administrative Privileges:
- Follow the principle of least privilege and only grant administrative privileges to users who require them for their job roles.
- Use separate administrative accounts for performing administrative tasks.

3. Regularly Update and Patch Systems:
- Keep AD servers, domain controllers, and other systems up to date with the latest security patches and updates.
- Implement a patch management process to ensure timely deployment of patches.

4. Monitor and Audit AD Activity:

- Enable auditing of critical AD events and regularly review audit logs for suspicious activity.
- Use tools like Microsoft Advanced Threat Analytics (ATA) or Azure Advanced Threat Protection (ATP) for real-time monitoring of AD activity.

5. Secure Domain Controllers:

- Physically secure domain controllers and restrict physical access to authorized personnel only.
- Enable BitLocker encryption for the system drive of domain controllers to protect data at rest.

6. Implement Group Policies:

- Use Group Policy to enforce security settings, such as account lockout policies, password policies, and user rights assignments.
- Regularly review and update Group Policy settings to align with security best practices.

7. Enable Firewall and Network Segmentation:

- Use firewalls to restrict inbound and outbound traffic to AD servers and domain controllers.
- Implement network segmentation to isolate AD infrastructure from other network segments.

8. Regularly Backup AD Data:

- Implement a regular backup strategy for AD data, including the AD database and system state.
- Store backups securely and test the restore process regularly.

9. Educate Users about Security:

- Provide security awareness training to users to help them recognize phishing attacks, malware, and other security threats.
- Encourage users to report suspicious activity to IT or security teams.

Encouraging users to report suspicious activity to IT or security teams is a key component of a strong security culture. Here are some ways to promote this behavior:

1. Training and Awareness:

- Provide regular security training and awareness sessions for employees to educate them about common security threats and how to recognize them.
- Emphasize the importance of reporting any unusual or suspicious activity promptly.

2. Clear Reporting Procedures:

- Establish clear and easy-to-follow procedures for reporting suspicious activity, including whom to contact and how to provide relevant information.
- Ensure that these procedures are well-known and easily accessible to all employees.

3. Anonymous Reporting:

- Offer anonymous reporting options to employees who may be hesitant to report suspicious activity for fear of retribution or other concerns.
- Anonymous reporting can encourage more people to come forward with information.

4. Promote a Positive Culture:

- Foster a positive and supportive culture around security, where reporting suspicious activity is seen as a responsible and valued behavior.
- Recognize and reward employees who report suspicious activity, either publicly or privately.

5. Lead by Example:

- Leaders and managers should lead by example by reporting any security concerns they encounter.
- This sets a precedent for the rest of the organization to follow.

6. Regular Communication:

- Regularly communicate with employees about the importance of reporting suspicious activity and provide updates on any security incidents or threats.
- Use multiple channels, such as emails, newsletters, posters, and meetings, to reinforce the message.

7. Feedback and Follow-Up:

- Provide feedback to employees who report suspicious activity, letting them know that their reports are taken seriously and acted upon.
- Follow up with employees to inform them of the outcome of their reports, if appropriate.

@ISSO.TECH.ENTERPRISES

By promoting a culture of security awareness and encouraging employees to report suspicious activity, you can help create a more secure environment for your organization.

10. Implement Security Updates and Best Practices:
- Stay informed about the latest security updates, best practices, and guidelines provided by Microsoft and other security organizations.

- Implement these updates and best practices to enhance the security of your AD environment.

By following these security best practices, you can help protect your organization's AD infrastructure from security threats and ensure the integrity and confidentiality of your data.

ISSO-TECH

VICTOR P HENDERSON | ISSO-TECH ENTERPRISES™
CERTIFIED ETHICAL HACKER C|EH

ISSO-TECH PRESS™

CHAPTER 19
POWERSHELL
TECHNIQUES

CHAPTER 19 | POWERSHELL TECHNIQUES
REMOTE DIAGNOSTICS

Using PowerShell for Active Directory diagnostics
PowerShell is a powerful tool for performing Active Directory (AD) diagnostics. Here's how you can use PowerShell for AD diagnostics:

1. Get-ADDomainController:
- Use the `Get-ADDomainController` cmdlet to retrieve information about domain controllers in the current domain or a specific domain.
Example:
```powershell
Get-ADDomainController -Filter *
```

2. Get-ADUser:
- Use the `Get-ADUser` cmdlet to retrieve information about AD users.
Example:
```powershell
Get-ADUser -Filter *
```

3. Get-ADGroup:
- Use the `Get-ADGroup` cmdlet to retrieve information about AD groups.
Example:
```powershell
Get-ADGroup -Filter *
```

4. Get-ADComputer:
- Use the `Get-ADComputer` cmdlet to retrieve information about AD computers.

VICTOR P HENDERSON | ISSO-TECH ENTERPRISES™
CERTIFIED ETHICAL HACKER C|EH

ISSO-TECH PRESS™

Example:
```powershell
Get-ADComputer -Filter *
```

5. Get-ADObject:

- Use the `Get-ADObject` cmdlet to retrieve information about any AD object.
Example:
```powershell
Get-ADObject -Filter *
```

6. Test-Connection:

- Use the `Test-Connection` cmdlet to test connectivity to a computer.
Example:
```powershell
Test-Connection -ComputerName "computername"
```

7. Get-EventLog:

- Use the `Get-EventLog` cmdlet to retrieve event log entries from a remote or local computer.
Example:
```powershell
Get-EventLog -LogName "Security" -EntryType "FailureAudit" -Newest 10
```

8. Get-WinEvent:

- Use the `Get-WinEvent` cmdlet to retrieve events from event logs based on various criteria.
Example:
```powershell
```


@ISSO.TECH.ENTERPRISES

```
Get-WinEvent        -LogName        "Security"        -FilterXPath
"*[System[(EventID=4625)]]"
```

9. Get-ADReplicationFailure:
- Use the `Get-ADReplicationFailure` cmdlet to retrieve information about AD replication failures.
Example:
```powershell
Get-ADReplicationFailure -Target REPDCA01 -Scope Domain
```

10. Get-ADReplicationPartnerMetadata:
- Use the `Get-ADReplicationPartnerMetadata` cmdlet to retrieve metadata for a specified replication partner.
Example:
```powershell
Get-ADReplicationPartnerMetadata -Target REPDCA01
```

These are just a few examples of how you can use PowerShell for AD diagnostics. PowerShell's flexibility and scripting capabilities make it a valuable tool for monitoring and troubleshooting AD environments.

- Analyzing Active Directory logs
Analyzing Active Directory (AD) logs is essential for maintaining security and troubleshooting issues. Here's how you can analyze AD logs using PowerShell:

1. Get-EventLog:
- Use the `Get-EventLog` cmdlet to retrieve AD-related events from the event logs.
Example:

```powershell
Get-EventLog -LogName Security -InstanceId 4625 -Newest 100 |
Format-List
```

This command retrieves the 100 most recent failed login attempts (Event ID 4625) from the Security log.

2. Get-WinEvent:
- Use the `Get-WinEvent` cmdlet for more advanced querying and filtering of event logs.
Example:
```powershell
Get-WinEvent          -LogName          Security          -FilterXPath
"*[System[EventID=4625]]" | Format-List
```

This command retrieves all failed login attempts (Event ID 4625) from the Security log.

3. Filtering by Date:
- You can filter events by date using the `-StartTime` and `-EndTime` parameters.
Example:
```powershell
Get-WinEvent          -LogName          Security          -FilterXPath
"*[System[EventID=4625]                                          and
System[TimeCreated[timediff(@SystemTime)  <=  86400000]]]"  |
Format-List
```

This command retrieves failed login attempts (Event ID 4625) from the last 24 hours.
4. Exporting to CSV:

@ISSO.TECH.ENTERPRISES

- You can export event log data to a CSV file for further analysis.
Example:
```powershell
Get-WinEvent -LogName Security -FilterXPath "*[System[EventID=4625]]" | Export-Csv -Path C:\Logs\FailedLogins.csv
```

This command exports all failed login attempts (Event ID 4625) from the Security log to a CSV file.

5. Advanced Filtering:
- Use XPath filters to perform more complex queries on event logs.
Example:
```powershell
Get-WinEvent -LogName Security -FilterXPath "*[System[EventID=4625] and EventData[Data[@Name='TargetUserName'] and (Data='username')]]" | Format-List
```

This command retrieves failed login attempts (Event ID 4625) for a specific username.

By using PowerShell to analyze AD logs, you can gain insights into security events, troubleshoot issues, and ensure the integrity of your AD environment.

- Troubleshooting complex Active Directory issues
Troubleshooting complex Active Directory (AD) issues requires a systematic approach and a good understanding of AD concepts. Here's a general framework for troubleshooting complex AD issues:

1. Define the Problem:
- Clearly define the symptoms of the issue and its impact on users or systems.
- Identify when the issue started and any recent changes that might be related.

2. Gather Information:
- Collect relevant information, such as error messages, event logs, and user reports.
- Use tools like Event Viewer, PowerShell cmdlets, and AD diagnostic tools to gather information.

3. Isolate the Issue:
- Determine if the issue is specific to a single user, computer, or AD object, or if it affects multiple users or systems.
- Use tools like Ping, NSLookup, and Test-Connection to check network connectivity and DNS resolution.

4. Check AD Replication:
- Ensure that AD replication is functioning correctly, especially if the issue involves multiple domain controllers.
- Use tools like Repadmin and AD Sites and Services to check replication status and topology.

5. Review AD Logs:
- Analyze AD logs for relevant events, such as authentication failures, replication errors, or directory service errors.
- Use PowerShell cmdlets like Get-EventLog and Get-WinEvent to review logs.

6. Check Group Policies:

- Verify that Group Policies are being applied correctly and are not causing the issue.
- Use tools like Group Policy Results or Group Policy Modeling to check policy settings.

7. Test Permissions:

- Verify that users have the necessary permissions to access resources in AD.
- Use tools like Effective Permissions or AccessEnum to test permissions.

8. Verify DNS Configuration:

- Ensure that DNS is configured correctly and that AD-related DNS records are present and resolving correctly.
- Use tools like NSLookup or DNS Manager to check DNS configuration.

9. Check for Network Issues:

- Verify that there are no network issues, such as latency or packet loss, that could be affecting AD communication.
- Use network troubleshooting tools to diagnose and resolve network issues.

10. Implement Solutions:

- Based on your analysis, implement solutions to address the underlying cause of the issue.
- Test the solutions to ensure they resolve the problem and do not cause any unintended consequences.

11. Document the Resolution:
- Document the steps taken to troubleshoot and resolve the issue.
- Update documentation and procedures to prevent similar issues in the future.

12. Monitor and Follow Up:
- Monitor the system to ensure that the issue has been resolved and that there are no recurrence.

- Follow up with users or stakeholders to verify that the problem has been resolved to their satisfaction.

By following this framework, you can effectively troubleshoot complex AD issues and ensure the stability and reliability of your AD environment.

@ISSO.TECH.ENTERPRISES

AUTOMATING ACTIVE DIRECTORY TASKS WITH POWERSHELL

Introduction to PowerShell Scripting

PowerShell scripting has emerged as an essential tool for IT professionals and network engineers, particularly in the context of managing Active Directory (AD) environments. As small businesses increasingly rely on efficient IT infrastructures, understanding PowerShell scripting not only enhances productivity but also streamlines complex administrative tasks. Its versatility allows for automation, reducing manual effort and minimizing the risk of human error, which is crucial for maintaining the integrity and security of Active Directory.

At its core, PowerShell is a task automation framework built on the .NET framework, enabling users to create scripts that can perform a wide array of functions. For those working with Active Directory, this means the capability to automate user account management, group policy updates, and security auditing processes. By mastering PowerShell, IT professionals can execute repetitive tasks with precision, allowing them to focus on more strategic initiatives, such as improving security best practices or planning for disaster recovery.

The integration of PowerShell with Active Directory is particularly beneficial when addressing the unique challenges associated with cloud environments. As businesses transition to hybrid infrastructures, the ability to manage both on-premises and cloud-based directories becomes paramount. PowerShell facilitates this integration seamlessly, enabling network engineers and system administrators to synchronize user accounts, manage permissions, and enforce compliance across multiple platforms without the need for extensive manual intervention.

Troubleshooting AD issues is another area where PowerShell scripting proves invaluable. With the right scripts, IT professionals can quickly diagnose problems related to authentication protocols or group policy application failures. The ability to automate these troubleshooting processes not only saves time but also ensures a more systematic approach to identifying and resolving issues, ultimately contributing to a more stable and secure Active Directory environment.

In summary, PowerShell scripting is a critical skill for any IT professional involved in managing Active Directory. Its capacity for automation enhances efficiency and accuracy, allowing for improved management of user accounts, security measures, and compliance mandates. As small businesses and IT teams navigate the complexities of modern network environments, mastering PowerShell scripting will undoubtedly position them for success in their Active Directory management endeavors.

@ISSO.TECH.ENTERPRISES

Common Active Directory Tasks for Automation

Active Directory (AD) serves as the backbone of identity management in many organizations, particularly within small businesses that rely on efficient user and resource management. As IT professionals, network engineers, and system engineers strive to optimize their workflows, automating common Active Directory tasks using PowerShell can significantly enhance productivity and accuracy. This subchapter delves into some of the most prevalent Active Directory tasks that are ripe for automation, illustrating how these practices can streamline operations while minimizing the potential for human error.

One of the most common tasks that can benefit from automation is user account management. Creating, modifying, and deleting user accounts can be a time-consuming process, especially in environments with frequent staff changes. By leveraging PowerShell scripts, IT professionals can automate the onboarding and offboarding processes, ensuring that user accounts are created or disabled in a consistent and timely manner. Scripts can be designed to pull data from CSV files, allowing for bulk account creation or updates. This not only saves time but also helps maintain compliance with internal security policies by ensuring that all necessary attributes are correctly populated.

Group management is another area where automation proves invaluable. Small businesses often have dynamic team structures, requiring frequent updates to group memberships. PowerShell enables administrators to automate the addition and removal of users from groups based on certain criteria, such as department or role changes. This process can be integrated with other systems, such as HR software, to ensure that group memberships are always aligned with current organizational needs. By automating group management tasks, IT professionals can reduce the risk of unauthorized access and enhance security posture.

Password management is a critical aspect of Active Directory that often involves repetitive tasks, such as resetting passwords for users. Automating password resets through PowerShell not only empowers users to manage their credentials but also alleviates the burden on IT staff. Self-service password reset tools can be implemented, allowing users to securely reset their passwords without direct intervention from IT. Additionally, scripts can be scheduled to enforce password policies, notify users of upcoming expirations, or even reset passwords en masse for compliance audits, thereby improving both efficiency and security.

Auditing and compliance are essential in any Active Directory environment, especially for small businesses that must adhere to various regulatory standards. Automating the auditing process using PowerShell can provide IT professionals with real-time insights into user activities, changes to group memberships, and modifications to critical objects within AD. By generating automated reports and alerts, organizations can proactively identify potential security threats and ensure compliance with industry regulations. This level of oversight not only enhances security but also helps in disaster recovery planning, as it provides a clear audit trail that can be referenced during investigations.

@ISSO.TECH.ENTERPRISES

In conclusion, automating common Active Directory tasks with PowerShell is an effective strategy for small businesses looking to enhance their IT operations. By focusing on user management, group administration, password management, and compliance auditing, organizations can significantly increase efficiency while reducing the risks associated with manual processes. As technology continues to evolve, embracing automation will not only streamline workflows but also empower IT professionals to focus on more strategic initiatives that drive business growth.

Advanced PowerShell Techniques for Active Directory

In the realm of Active Directory management, PowerShell has emerged as an indispensable tool, particularly for small businesses and IT professionals looking to streamline their operations. This subchapter explores advanced PowerShell techniques that enhance efficiency and security within Active Directory environments. By mastering these techniques, network and system engineers can not only automate routine tasks but also implement robust security measures, optimize group policy management, and facilitate smooth migrations to cloud environments.

One of the key advanced techniques involves leveraging PowerShell scripts to perform bulk operations on Active Directory objects. For instance, administrators can use the Get-ADUser and Set-ADUser cmdlets in conjunction with pipeline commands to efficiently update user attributes across multiple accounts. This bulk processing capability is particularly beneficial for businesses that experience high turnover rates or those that regularly onboard new employees. By utilizing these scripts, IT professionals can ensure that user information is consistently up to date, thereby enhancing both compliance and security.

In addition to bulk operations, PowerShell can be used to implement advanced auditing and compliance strategies. By employing the Get-EventLog cmdlet alongside event filters, administrators can create customized reports that track changes to Active Directory objects. This not only aids in meeting regulatory requirements but also helps in identifying potential security breaches. Integrating these auditing techniques with regular reporting schedules can empower small business IT teams to proactively monitor their environments, ensuring that any anomalies are addressed promptly.

Security best practices are paramount in any Active Directory deployment, and PowerShell can be a powerful ally in enforcing these practices. Utilizing cmdlets such as Get-ADGroupMember and Remove-ADGroupMember, administrators can regularly audit group memberships to prevent privilege creep. Furthermore, advanced scripting techniques can automate the review process, generating alerts when unauthorized changes are detected. This level of vigilance not only safeguards sensitive data but also fosters a culture of accountability within the organization.

Lastly, as organizations increasingly migrate to cloud environments, integrating Active Directory with services like Azure AD becomes essential. PowerShell provides several cmdlets designed specifically for this purpose, allowing seamless synchronization of on-premises directories with cloud-based services. By implementing these advanced techniques, IT professionals can ensure that their Active Directory remains a central component of their identity management strategy, effectively bridging the gap between on-premises and cloud environments. This integration not only enhances operational efficiency but also ensures that security protocols are uniformly applied across all platforms.

In conclusion, advanced PowerShell techniques offer a wealth of opportunities for small businesses and IT professionals to enhance their Active Directory management. From automating routine tasks and enforcing security best practices to facilitating cloud integration and compliance auditing, these techniques are essential for optimizing Active Directory environments. By mastering these skills, network and system engineers can significantly improve their operational efficiency and ensure that their Active Directory implementations are robust, secure, and aligned with business objectives.

ISSO-TECH

VICTOR P HENDERSON | ISSO-TECH ENTERPRISES™
CERTIFIED ETHICAL HACKER C|EH

ISSO-TECH PRESS™

229.320.151.8

CHAPTER 20
THE BOOK OF KNOWLEDGE

CHAPTER 20 | THE BOOK OF KNOWLEDGE
REAL-WORLD SCENARIOS

The Book of Knowledge offers a unique blend of hands-on training directly from Microsoft, deep insights and knowledge gained as an ethical hacker, with years of extensive real-world experience working with Active Directory. This resource is crafted to elevate your understanding of enterprise IT management, focusing on essential practices that enhance security and operational efficiency.

Essential Security Principle: Never leave any configuration at its default settings. Default configurations create vulnerabilities that invite hackers to exploit weaknesses in your data infrastructure. This knowledge, familiar to IT professionals worldwide, is foundational to securing any information system, whether for a small business or a large enterprise.

With that in mind, consider the following recommendations:

Structuring Active Directory for Organizational Efficiency

As the IT professional in your enterprise, configure Active Directory to mirror your company's organizational structure. Organize your Organizational Units (OUs), user accounts, and security groups to reflect departmental divisions. This alignment promotes centralized security and simplifies management.

1. **Separate User Types**: Place temporary and part-time users in distinct groups from permanent, full-time employees. This setup enables you to apply expiration dates for

seasonal staff, contractors, and temporary personnel directly in Active Directory.

2. **Secure Shared Resources**: When configuring shared resources, assign security groups rather than individual users. Managing access through security groups streamlines permissions across multiple shared resources, ensuring easier management.

3. **Principle of Least Privilege**: Grant users only the necessary authority to perform their roles. Limiting user permissions minimizes privilege escalation risks, safeguarding proprietary data from unauthorized access by potential bad actors.

4. **Tailor Your Directory Naming**: Rename elements such as Active Directory Schema, Forest, Sites, and Domains from defaults like "Default-First-Site" to identifiers specific to your business. This step helps protect your environment by aligning it with your organization's identity.

④ISSO.TECH.ENTERPRISES

Tech Tips for Active Directory Optimization

Tech Tip #1: Organize Your Systems
When creating OUs, include specific ones for servers and workstations.

This separation allows better control over security updates and patch management.

Tech Tip #2: Expand Active Directory Beyond Windows
Active Directory isn't just for Windows systems. Include OUs for network devices and Linux systems as well.

While you may not be able to push updates to all devices, this method aids in network audits and inventory tracking. For budget-conscious organizations, Active Directory can serve as a viable inventory tool when third-party solutions are cost-prohibitive.

Tech Tip #3: Establish Standardized Naming Conventions
Standardize naming conventions for data-center servers and workstations by department, function, OS, or location for consistency and streamlined management.

Server Naming Example

- ➢ **WINFSHRNY1:** Windows, File Server, Human Resources, New York, Server #1
- ➢ **LXDCHQLA5:** Linux, Domain Controller, Headquarters, Los Angeles, Server #5

229.320.151.8

Workstation Naming Example

- ➢ **WINGRXJDNY:** Windows, Graphics Department, John Doe, New York
- ➢ **LXITJDMI:** Linux, IT Department, Jane Doe, Miami

Tech Tip #4: Implement Group Policy Objects (GPOs) Wisely

Use GPOs to enforce security settings across user accounts and workstations, including password policies, screen lock timers, and access restrictions. Limit GPO scope to prevent configuration conflicts, and apply policies at the OU level when possible for finer control.

Tech Tip #5: Enable Auditing and Logging

Regularly monitor logs for unauthorized access attempts and unusual activity within Active Directory. Use advanced auditing features to track user logons, group changes, and privilege escalations. This practice is critical for early detection of potential security breaches.

Tech Tip #6: Use Role-Based Access Control (RBAC)

Organize permissions based on user roles within the company rather than assigning privileges individually. RBAC ensures consistency and limits access based on job requirements, reducing the risk of unauthorized access.

Tech Tip #7: Disable Inactive Accounts Regularly

Run regular audits to identify inactive accounts and disable them to reduce potential attack vectors. For temporary or seasonal staff, automate account expiration dates as part of the account setup process.

Tech Tip #8: Implement Multi-Factor Authentication (MFA)

Add an extra layer of security by enabling MFA for access to Active Directory, VPNs, and other critical systems. MFA adds a strong barrier against unauthorized access, particularly for remote users.

Tech Tip #9: Set Up Conditional Access Policies

For users accessing systems remotely, use conditional access to restrict access based on factors like geographic location, device type, and IP address. This minimizes unauthorized access by allowing only verified users to log in.

Tech Tip #10: Optimize DNS Settings for Active Directory

Active Directory relies heavily on DNS. Ensure your DNS servers are redundant and configured for fast failover to maintain reliable connectivity. Implement DNS security extensions (DNSSEC) to prevent spoofing and other DNS attacks.

Tech Tip #11: Utilize Password Vaults for Admin Accounts

Store admin passwords securely in a password vault and limit access to authorized IT staff only. Regularly rotate these passwords and enforce multi-factor authentication for vault access.

Tech Tip #12: Automate Permissions Management Using PowerShell Scripts

VICTOR P HENDERSON | ISSO-TECH ENTERPRISES™
CERTIFIED ETHICAL HACKER C|EH

ISSO-TECH PRESS™

PowerShell scripting can automate repetitive tasks, such as user provisioning, OU structure changes, and permissions management. Schedule scripts to update permissions, check account statuses, and monitor for anomalies without manual intervention.

I take a deep dive into this topic within my new book titled: The Book of Powershell available at all online book retailers.

Tech Tip #13: Regularly Test and Review Backup and Restore Processes

Ensure Active Directory has frequent backups that are securely stored. Test the restore process regularly to verify it works effectively, as this is essential for rapid recovery in the event of data corruption or system failure.

Tech Tip #14: Enforce Strong Password Policies

Configure strong password requirements across all accounts. Enforce a mix of characters, minimum length, and regular changes, and consider using password history to prevent users from reusing old passwords.

Tech Tip #15: Limit Admin Accounts with Domain-Wide Privileges

Keep the number of domain administrator accounts to a minimum and apply stringent monitoring on these accounts. Assign domain-wide privileges sparingly, as these accounts are prime targets for malicious actors.

Tech Tip #16: Use Restricted Groups for Elevated Permissions

@ISSO.TECH.ENTERPRISES

Implement restricted groups for users requiring elevated permissions. This practice simplifies the management of admin privileges by automatically adding or removing users from groups based on their assigned roles.

Tech Tip #17: Segment Your Network by Security Level

Separate network segments based on sensitivity levels (e.g., production, testing, guest). This helps to contain breaches and protects sensitive data by limiting unauthorized access between segments.

Tech Tip #18: Create Service Accounts with Minimal Privileges

Service accounts should be created with only the privileges necessary for their specific task. Avoid using admin accounts for service operations to prevent escalation risks if the service is compromised.

Tech Tip #19: Configure Data Encryption for Sensitive Information

For highly sensitive data, enforce encryption on both stored data and data in transit. Active Directory's Kerberos protocol provides encryption for authentication, but additional file-level encryption protects proprietary data from unauthorized access.

229.320.151.8

Copyrighted Material

Each of these tips adds layers of security, control, and efficiency to your Active Directory environment, empowering your business to safeguard data, streamline IT operations, and maintain organizational integrity.

The Book of Knowledge stands as a powerful resource for IT professionals, offering actionable insights to secure, manage, and optimize enterprise systems effectively.

Real-world examples of Active Directory diagnostics
Active Directory (AD) diagnostics are crucial for maintaining a healthy AD environment. Here are some real-world examples:

1. Replication Issues: Monitoring replication health is essential. Tools like Repadmin can be used to check replication status and diagnose any issues.

2. Authentication Problems: Monitoring authentication requests and failures can help identify issues with domain controllers or user accounts. Event Viewer can be used to view relevant logs.

3. DNS Configuration: Incorrect DNS settings can cause various AD issues. Tools like DCDiag can be used to diagnose DNS-related problems.

4. Group Policy Issues: Group Policy problems can cause inconsistent settings across the network. Tools like GPResult can help diagnose and troubleshoot Group Policy application issues.

5. Trust Relationship Problems: Trust relationships between domains can sometimes break, causing authentication issues. Netdom or PowerShell commands can be used to diagnose and repair trust relationships.

6. AD Database Corruption: AD database corruption can cause serious issues. Tools like NTDSUtil can be used to check for and repair database corruption.

7. LDAP Errors: Monitoring LDAP queries and errors can help identify issues with LDAP authentication or queries.

8. AD Replication Latency: Monitoring replication latency can help ensure that changes are replicated in a timely manner across all domain controllers.

9. Expired Certificates: Expired certificates can cause authentication failures. Monitoring certificate expiration dates can help prevent this issue.

10. Security Auditing: Regularly auditing AD for security events can help identify potential security issues or unauthorized access attempts.

Implementing these diagnostic practices can help maintain a healthy and secure Active Directory environment.
- Best practices based on case studies

Based on case studies and real-world experiences, here are some best practices for managing Active Directory (AD) environments:

1. Regular Monitoring and Maintenance: Regularly monitor the health and performance of your AD environment using tools like Performance Monitor, Event Viewer, and third-party monitoring solutions.

2. Regular Backups: Implement a regular backup strategy for AD, including system state backups, to ensure you can recover in case of data loss or corruption.
3. Patch Management: Stay up to date with Windows updates and patches to protect against security vulnerabilities and ensure system stability.

4. Security Best Practices: Implement security best practices such as strong password policies, regular audits, least privilege access, and monitoring for suspicious activity.

5. Group Policy Management: Use Group Policy to enforce security settings, software deployment, and other configurations consistently across your AD environment.

6. Regular Audits: Conduct regular audits of your AD environment to ensure compliance with security policies and to identify and remediate any issues.

7. Monitor Replication: Monitor AD replication to ensure changes are being replicated correctly across all domain controllers and sites.

8. Capacity Planning: Monitor and plan for the growth of your AD environment to ensure it can handle increasing loads and user accounts.

9. Disaster Recovery Planning: Develop and regularly test a disaster recovery plan to ensure you can recover your AD environment in case of a major outage or disaster.

10. Training and Documentation: Provide training to IT staff on AD best practices and maintain up-to-date documentation of your AD environment's configuration and procedures.

Implementing these best practices can help ensure the stability, security, and performance of your Active Directory environment.
- Lessons learned from troubleshooting Active Directory issues

Troubleshooting Active Directory (AD) issues can be complex, but it often provides valuable lessons. Here are some key lessons learned from troubleshooting AD problems:

1. Understand the Basics: Having a solid understanding of how AD works, including its components (e.g., domains, domain controllers, trusts) and how they interact, is crucial for effective troubleshooting.

2. Logs Are Your Friend: AD generates a variety of logs (e.g., Event Viewer, replication logs) that can provide valuable information for troubleshooting. Learning to interpret these logs is essential.

3. Replication Is Critical: AD replication is fundamental to its operation. Understanding how replication works and monitoring its health can help prevent and resolve many issues.

4. Check DNS: DNS issues are a common cause of AD problems. Ensuring that DNS is properly configured and resolving correctly is essential.

5. Use the Right Tools: Windows Server includes several tools (e.g., DCDiag, Repadmin, Event Viewer) specifically designed for troubleshooting AD. Learning to use these tools effectively is key.

6. Isolate the Problem: Troubleshooting often involves isolating the issue to a specific component or process. This can help narrow down the possible causes and solutions.

7. Test Changes Carefully: When making changes to AD (e.g., adding or removing domain controllers, changing group policies), it's important to test them in a controlled environment before applying them in production.

8. Document Everything: Keeping detailed documentation of your AD environment, including configurations, changes, and troubleshooting steps, can help you quickly resolve future issues.

9. Stay Calm and Patient: AD troubleshooting can be challenging and time-consuming. Maintaining a calm and patient approach can help you stay focused and find solutions more effectively.

10. Learn from Each Issue: Every AD issue provides an opportunity to learn and improve your troubleshooting skills. Take the time to reflect on each problem and how you resolved it, so you can be better prepared for future challenges.

By applying these lessons learned, you can become more effective at troubleshooting Active Directory issues and maintaining a stable and reliable AD environment.

ISSO-TECH

VICTOR P HENDERSON | ISSO-TECH ENTERPRISES™
CERTIFIED ETHICAL HACKER C|EH

ISSO-TECH PRESS™

229.320.151.8

CHAPTER 21
DIAGNOSTIC BEST PRACTICES

CHAPTER 21 | DIAGNOSTIC BEST PRACTICES
TRENDS

Emerging trends in Active Directory diagnostics

Emerging trends in Active Directory (AD) diagnostics are focused on enhancing security, improving performance, and simplifying management. Some of the key trends include:

1. Cloud Integration: As organizations adopt hybrid and multi-cloud environments, there is a growing trend towards integrating on-premises AD with cloud-based identity and access management solutions. This trend requires new diagnostic tools and practices to ensure seamless integration and security.

2. Zero Trust Security: The Zero Trust security model, which assumes that every access attempt is potentially malicious and requires verification, is gaining traction. AD diagnostics are evolving to support Zero Trust principles, such as continuous authentication and least privilege access.

3. Identity Governance: Identity governance solutions are becoming more sophisticated, requiring AD diagnostics to provide insights into user access rights, permissions, and compliance with security policies.

4. Machine Learning and AI: Machine learning and AI are being used to analyze AD logs and detect anomalies that may indicate security threats or performance issues. These technologies can help organizations proactively identify and mitigate potential problems.

ISSO-TECH PRESS™

5.   Containerization: As organizations adopt containerized applications, AD diagnostics are adapting to monitor and manage identity and access within container environments.

6. DevOps Integration: AD diagnostics are being integrated into DevOps processes to automate the deployment and management of AD configurations, improving agility and reducing manual errors.

7. Improved Reporting and Visualization: There is a trend towards providing more intuitive and actionable insights through improved reporting and visualization tools, making it easier for administrators to identify and resolve issues.

8. Enhanced Compliance Reporting: With increasing regulatory requirements, AD diagnostics are evolving to provide more comprehensive compliance reporting, helping organizations demonstrate adherence to security and privacy standards.

9. Mobile Device Management (MDM) Integration: As more organizations embrace mobile devices in the workplace, AD diagnostics are integrating with MDM solutions to manage user identities and access on mobile devices securely.

10. Edge Computing: AD diagnostics are evolving to support edge computing environments, ensuring that identity and access management functions are optimized for distributed edge devices and networks.
Overall, the trend in AD diagnostics is towards greater integration, automation, and intelligence, enabling organizations to enhance security, improve performance, and streamline management of their AD environments.

- Best practices for maintaining a healthy Active Directory environment

Maintaining a healthy Active Directory (AD) environment is crucial for ensuring the security, stability, and performance of your organization's IT infrastructure. Here are some best practices for keeping your AD environment in top shape:

1. Regular Backups: Perform regular backups of your AD database and system state to protect against data loss in case of hardware failure, accidental deletion, or other disasters.

2. Monitor AD Health: Use tools like Event Viewer, Performance Monitor, and AD-specific monitoring tools to regularly check the health and performance of your AD environment.

3. Patch Management: Keep your AD servers up to date with the latest security patches and updates from Microsoft to protect against vulnerabilities.

4. Security Best Practices: Implement security best practices such as strong password policies, least privilege access, regular audits, and monitoring for suspicious activity to protect against security threats.

5. Regular Maintenance: Perform regular maintenance tasks such as cleaning up stale accounts, checking for and resolving replication issues, and monitoring disk space usage.

6. Monitor Replication: Monitor AD replication to ensure that changes are being replicated correctly across all domain controllers.

7. DNS Health: Ensure that your DNS infrastructure is healthy and properly configured, as AD heavily relies on DNS for its operation.

8. Group Policy Management: Regularly review and update Group Policy settings to ensure that they are applied correctly and consistently across your AD environment.

9. Capacity Planning: Monitor the growth of your AD environment and plan for additional resources (e.g., domain controllers, storage) as needed to ensure scalability and performance.

10. Regular Audits: Conduct regular audits of your AD environment to ensure compliance with security policies and to identify and remediate any issues.

11. Training and Documentation: Provide training to IT staff on AD best practices and maintain up-to-date documentation of your AD environment's configuration and procedures.

By following these best practices, you can help ensure that your Active Directory environment remains healthy, secure, and efficient, providing a solid foundation for your organization's IT operations.

- Conclusion and final thoughts
Maintaining a healthy Active Directory environment is essential for the overall security and efficiency of an organization's IT infrastructure. By implementing best practices such as regular backups, monitoring, patch management, and security measures, organizations can mitigate risks and ensure the smooth operation of their AD environment.

It's also important to stay informed about emerging trends and technologies in AD diagnostics and management, as these can help organizations adapt to evolving security threats and IT requirements. Additionally, ongoing training and documentation are key to ensuring that IT staff are equipped to effectively manage and troubleshoot AD issues.

In conclusion, by following best practices, staying proactive, and continuously improving their AD management strategies, organizations can maintain a healthy and secure Active Directory environment that meets the needs of their users and business operations.

This book provides a comprehensive guide to diagnosing and troubleshooting Microsoft Active Directory issues, covering everything from performance monitoring to disaster recovery. It is designed for IT professionals, system administrators, and anyone responsible for managing Active Directory in their organization.

CONCLUSION AND NEXT STEPS

Recap of Key Concepts

In this subchapter, we will recap the essential concepts covered throughout the book "Automating Active Directory Tasks with PowerShell: Boosting Efficiency for IT Professionals." Our focus has been on providing practical insights and tools that can significantly enhance the management and security of Active Directory (AD) within small businesses and among IT professionals. Understanding these key concepts is crucial for ensuring efficient operations, especially in environments that are increasingly dependent on cloud solutions and require robust security measures.

One of the central themes discussed is the importance of mastering Active Directory itself. This foundational knowledge enables IT professionals, network engineers, and system engineers to navigate the complexities of user management, access controls, and group policies effectively. By understanding the structure and function of AD, professionals can implement best practices that not only streamline administrative tasks but also bolster the security of the organization's IT infrastructure. This involves leveraging group policies for consistent security settings across the network, which is vital for maintaining compliance with industry regulations.

Security best practices for Active Directory have also been a prominent topic. Given the rise in cyber threats and the critical role that AD plays in authenticating users and managing resources, implementing stringent security measures is non-negotiable. The book emphasizes strategies such as regular audits, the principle of least privilege, and the importance of monitoring access logs to detect anomalies. By adopting these practices, small businesses can mitigate risks and ensure that their Active Directory environments remain secure against potential breaches.

As organizations transition to cloud environments, integrating Active Directory with Azure AD is becoming increasingly relevant. This integration allows for seamless identity management across on-premises and cloud applications, enabling businesses to take full advantage of cloud features while maintaining control over user access. The book outlines the steps necessary for successful integration, focusing on synchronization of identities and enabling single sign-on capabilities, which enhance user experience and security alike.

Lastly, the book emphasizes the significance of automation in managing Active Directory tasks using PowerShell. Automation not only improves efficiency but also reduces the potential for human error. We explored various scripts and commands that can be employed to automate routine tasks such as user provisioning, group membership changes, and compliance reporting. By leveraging these automation techniques, IT professionals can focus their efforts on strategic initiatives rather than getting bogged down by repetitive administrative tasks. The integration of these concepts into daily operations can lead to significant improvements in productivity and overall IT governance.

Future Trends in Active Directory Management

As we move deeper into the era of digital transformation, the management of Active Directory (AD) is evolving rapidly, driven by advancements in technology and changing business needs. For small businesses and IT professionals, understanding these trends is crucial for maintaining a robust and secure IT infrastructure. One significant trend is the increased integration of Active Directory with cloud services, particularly Azure Active Directory (Azure AD). This integration not only enhances scalability and flexibility but also allows organizations to leverage cloud-based identity and access management features that can streamline operations.

Another notable trend is the growing emphasis on security best practices within Active Directory environments. As cyber threats continue to rise, small businesses must prioritize AD security measures. The adoption of Zero Trust security models is becoming more prevalent, requiring organizations to rethink their authentication strategies. This includes the implementation of multi-factor authentication (MFA) and conditional access policies, which can help mitigate risks associated with user credentials and enhance overall security posture.

Automation through PowerShell is also set to play a pivotal role in the future of Active Directory management. As IT professionals seek to boost efficiency, the ability to automate routine tasks, such as user provisioning, password resets, and group policy updates, will become increasingly important. This trend not only reduces the potential for human error but also frees up valuable time for IT teams to focus on higher-value initiatives. Organizations that embrace PowerShell automation will likely see significant improvements in operational efficiency and resource allocation.

In addition to automation, the management of Active Directory will increasingly incorporate advanced analytics and machine learning. By leveraging these technologies, organizations can gain deeper insights into user behavior and network activity, enabling proactive identification of anomalies and potential security threats. This predictive approach to AD management can lead to more informed decision-making and a stronger defense against cyber incidents, positioning small businesses to better protect their assets and data.

Finally, as compliance and auditing requirements continue to evolve, the need for rigorous monitoring and reporting within Active Directory will become more pronounced. Organizations will be compelled to adopt comprehensive auditing and compliance frameworks to ensure adherence to industry standards and regulations. This trend will require IT professionals to develop new strategies for tracking changes, managing permissions, and producing reports that demonstrate compliance. By staying ahead of these trends, small businesses can not only enhance their Active Directory management practices but also ensure long-term sustainability and security in an increasingly complex digital landscape.

Resources for Continued Learning

In the ever-evolving landscape of IT, particularly regarding Active Directory (AD) management and automation with PowerShell, continuous learning is paramount for small businesses, IT professionals, network engineers, and system engineers. As the demands of technology grow, so too must the skills of those who manage it. To help you stay ahead in mastering Active Directory and related tasks, a variety of resources are available, ranging from online courses and forums to books and certification programs.

Online platforms such as Pluralsight, LinkedIn Learning, and Udemy offer a plethora of courses specifically tailored to Active Directory topics, including security best practices, group policy management, and cloud integration with Azure AD. These courses often feature hands-on labs and real-world scenarios that allow you to apply what you learn immediately. Moreover, many platforms provide the opportunity to earn certificates, which can enhance your professional credentials and demonstrate your commitment to ongoing education.

For those seeking a more interactive learning environment, community forums and discussion groups can be invaluable. Websites like Spiceworks, TechNet, and Reddit host vibrant communities where IT professionals share insights, troubleshoot issues, and discuss the latest trends in Active Directory management. Participating in these forums not only helps you solve current challenges but also expands your network and allows you to learn from the experiences of others in the field.

Books specifically focused on Active Directory and PowerShell automation remain a crucial resource for in-depth understanding. Titles such as "Active Directory: Designing, Deploying, and Running Active Directory" and "Learn Windows PowerShell in a Month of Lunches" provide comprehensive knowledge that can enhance your skills significantly. Reading these books can solidify your understanding of complex topics like Active Directory migration strategies, disaster recovery planning, and compliance auditing, enabling you to implement best practices effectively in your organization.

Finally, pursuing industry-recognized certifications can significantly bolster your expertise while providing structured learning paths. Certifications such as Microsoft Certified: Azure Administrator Associate or Microsoft Certified: Windows Server Hybrid Administrator Associate are excellent options for validating your skills in integrating Active Directory with Azure AD and managing hybrid environments. By investing time in these resources and certifications, you can ensure that you remain proficient in Active Directory management and automation, thereby enhancing the efficiency and security of your organization's IT infrastructure.

ISSO-TECH

VICTOR P HENDERSON | ISSO-TECH ENTERPRISES™
CERTIFIED ETHICAL HACKER C|EH

ISSO-TECH PRESS™

EPILOGUE

EPILOGUE | MASTERING ACTIVE DIRECTORY
ISSO-TECH ENTERPRISES™

As we conclude our journey through "Mastering Active Directory," it is fitting to reflect on the vast landscape we've navigated together. This book has provided an in-depth exploration of Active Directory, offering insights that are both profound and practical. From understanding fundamental concepts to mastering advanced configurations, our goal has been to equip you with the knowledge and skills necessary to leverage this powerful tool effectively.

Active Directory is not merely a directory service; it is the backbone of many IT infrastructures, essential for managing identities, resources, and security in today's complex digital environments. The principles and techniques discussed in this book are intended to help you navigate the intricacies of Active Directory with confidence and precision.

Throughout these pages, we have delved into the architecture of Active Directory, explored strategies for optimal deployment and management, and tackled real-world scenarios that illustrate the dynamic nature of this technology. The expertise you have gained will undoubtedly serve as a cornerstone in your professional toolkit, enabling you to design, implement, and maintain robust directory services that drive organizational success.

It is essential to remember that technology is ever-evolving, and so too must our understanding and application of it. As you continue to expand your knowledge and experience in the field of IT, let the principles outlined in this book guide you in adapting to new

VICTOR P HENDERSON | ISSO-TECH ENTERPRISES™
CERTIFIED ETHICAL HACKER C|EH

ISSO-TECH PRESS™

challenges and opportunities. Embrace the continuous learning that comes with advancements in technology and stay abreast of emerging trends and best practices.

I hope that this book has not only enhanced your technical acumen but also inspired a deeper appreciation for the critical role that Active Directory plays in modern IT environments. The journey of mastering such a complex and integral system is ongoing, and the pursuit of excellence in this field is a testament to your dedication and expertise.

Thank you for embarking on this journey with me. May your continued exploration of Active Directory bring you success and fulfillment in your endeavors.

- VICTOR P. HENDERSON –
CERTIFIED ETHICAL HACKER C|EH

ISSO-TECH

VICTOR P HENDERSON | ISSO-TECH ENTERPRISES™
CERTIFIED ETHICAL HACKER C|EH

ISSO-TECH PRESS™

229.320.151.8

BIOGRAPHY

BIOGRAPHY | VICTOR P HENDERSON
CERTIFIED ETHICAL HACKER | C|EH

Victor P. Henderson is a seasoned IT professional and a leading authority in the field of network and cyber security. With over 20 years of experience, he has navigated the rapidly evolving landscape of technology, consistently staying ahead of the curve. His expertise spans a wide range of areas, including ethical hacking, IT security engineering, and Cisco network management.

Henderson holds multiple professional IT certifications, a testament to his commitment to continuous learning and professional growth. He is a Certified Ethical Hacker, a credential that speaks volumes about his deep understanding of how to identify vulnerabilities and secure systems. As an IT Security Engineer, he has developed and implemented robust security protocols for numerous enterprise organizations. His role as a Cisco Network Professional has ushered him forward to architect, implement, and manage complex network infrastructures, further honing his skills in network security.

His book, "Defensive Ethical Hacking: Techniques, Strategies, and Defense Tactics", is a reflection of his extensive knowledge and experience. It serves as a comprehensive guide for IT professionals and enthusiasts, providing insights into the world of ethical hacking and network security.

Henderson's career is marked by a relentless pursuit of knowledge and a deep desire to help others navigate the complex world of IT

ISSO-TECH PRESS™

229.320.151.8

security. His insights and strategies are invaluable to anyone looking to fortify their digital defenses. His commitment to his field and his passion for sharing his knowledge make him a respected figure in the IT community.

SOCIAL MEDIA: @ISSO.TECH.ENTERPRISES
WEBSITE: WWW.ISSOTECHENTERPRISES.COM

© **MASTERING ACTIVE DIRECTORY**

@ISSO.TECH.ENTERPRISES

ISSO-TECH

VICTOR P HENDERSON | ISSO-TECH ENTERPRISES™
CERTIFIED ETHICAL HACKER C|EH

ISSO-TECH PRESS™

229.320.151.6

ABOUT THE PUBLISHER

ABOUT THE PUBLISHER | ISSO-TECH PRESS™,
"Empowering Minds Through Innovative Information Technology
Publishing"...

WEBSITE: HTTPS://WWW.ISSOTECHENTERPRISES.COM
SOCIAL MEDIA: @ISSO.TECH.ENTERPRISES

ISSO-TECH PRESS™, "Empowering Minds Through Innovative
Information Technology Publishing"...

At ISSO-TECH PRESS™, we provide a platform for tech-savvy
authors, writers, visionaries and innovators to fully express
themselves and share their groundbreaking ideas. Our mission is to
bring you the most insightful and transformative books in the world
of information technology.

We empower experts to convey their knowledge and creativity,
delivering profound and cutting-edge tech stories and insights. With
ISSO-TECH PRESS™, immerse yourself in the forefront of
technological innovation and exploration.

ISSO-TECH PRESS™

229.320.151.8

***©DEFENSIVE ETHICAL HACKING**
TECHNIQUES STRATEGIES AND DEFENSE TACTICS

***©CISCO NETWORKS FOR NEW ENGINEERS**
TECHNIQUES, STRATEGIES, AND TACTICS

***©AI FOR SMALL BUSINESS**
ARTIFICIAL INTELLIGENCE HARNESING AI FOR SMALL
BUSINESS

***©MASTERING ACTIVE DIRECTORY**
DIRECTORY SERVICES, SECURITY & INFRASTRUCTURE
MANAGEMENT

***©THE BOOK OF POWERSHELL**
AUTOMATION, SCRIPTING, AND REMOTE IT
MANAGEMENT FOR WINDOWS

229.320.151.8